T0149729

Devour Obstacles for Dinner

Tools to Develop a Fearless Attitude, Discover Joy, and Achieve Goals

ROBIN RAE MORRIS

BALBOA.
PRESS
A DIVISION OF HAY HOUSE

Balboa Press books may be ordered through booksellers or by contacting:

Balboa Press
A Division of Hay House
1663 Liberty Drive
Bloomington, IN 47403
www.balboapress.com
1 (877) 407-4847

Print information available on the last page.

ISBN: 978-1-5043-4586-6 (sc)
ISBN: 978-1-5043-4588-0 (hc)
ISBN: 978-1-5043-4587-3 (e)

Library of Congress Control Number: 2016900578

Balboa Press rev. date: 9/26/2016

Contents

Part Four: Counseling Can Help You Ask Important Questions

Part Five: Counseling Can Help You Improve Your Relationships

Part Six: Counseling Can Provide Engaging Metaphors

Deepest appreciation goes to my mentors, JoAnne Averett, Dr. Daisaku Ikeda, Dr. Deborah Walters, and each client who shared his or her amazing story with me.

Love and gratitude go to all those who gave me endless encouragement, especially Mom, Kev, Gina, Susan, Linda, Wendi, Carrie, Melissa, Wendy, and Chris.

Sarah, for all of your love and care; there is not enough chocolate and fluffy nougat in the world to properly thank you.

Allie, heartfelt thanks to you for your ability to find the clearest and snappiest turns of phrase.

And last but never least, thanks to Dad, who calmed a million fears with three words: "Things work out."

Preface

Do you feel stuck in a relationship, in your career, or in a specific area of your life? Are you constantly wrestling with the question "should I stay, or should I go?" Do you have a great life on paper but maintain a vague yet unshakeable feeling that your life could be more fulfilling? Do you yearn to have more meaningful connections and a deeper sense of purpose in life? Are you limited by anxiety, panic attacks, or depression? Have you worked so hard for so long that you're no longer able to refuel your passion for life? Do you feel that joy in life is something only other people get? Is there a situation, event, or diagnosis that has rocked your world in a way that you've never been shaken before?

Could you use a little help sorting all of this out—not in some theoretical way but with practical tools to help you make important changes and meet your challenges head on?

For the last twenty years, I've been working on a set of tools to help my clients answer these questions. After a while, I started to get the same request over and over from different people in different areas of my life: "Can I get a written copy of all the tools you talk about?"

Now I can finally say yes!

The tools in this book correspond to inspirational stories of individuals who have transformed their struggles - that is, each person was able to use his or her issues, problems, and hardships to discover how strong and resilient they really are, and then discover deeper joy in life as they fulfilled their goals. Sometimes, without even being fully aware of it, each person developed a fearless attitude as s/he figured out how to devour obstacles for dinner.

And you can too!

If you or someone you know is struggling, this book can provide both answers and inspiration. If you're a therapist, you'll find new tools to reignite your passion for helping others.

In these pages, you'll find a friend to encourage and support you. You'll be inspired to make a unique contribution to your family, friends, community, and career and to this beautiful, blue planet. This book exists to serve you. Now make it your own.

Part One: Meet and Greet

Ridin' in the Atommobile

Standing in a line at Disneyland with Mickey Mouse ears atop my head, I stared—equally scared and fascinated—at a ride called Adventures through Inner Space. I instinctively slipped my small, six-year-old hand into my father's large palm as we watched the riders in front of us take their seats in the Atommobile—a converted car that carried visitors down a dark tunnel. We stood at one end of the Mighty Microscope and peered through a glass tube, which showed the Atommobile traveling farther and farther away. Then it was our turn. Once seated in the Atommobile, I clung to my father's arm, and we drove down the tunnel. In the darkness, the voice of an unseen scientist told us we had "passed beyond the limits of normal Mag-ni-fi-ca-tion." In other words, we were shrinking to the size of microscopic molecules!

As we entered through the tunnel, delicate snowflakes fluttered down around us, but as we continued, they grew larger and larger. The scientist said, "Although your body will shrink, your mind will expand." I watched wide-eyed and delighted as the snowflakes progressively grew to two hundred times the size of a little girl—a single snowflake became large enough to fill my entire field of vision. I was surrounded by infinite uniqueness and immeasurable beauty unfolding in every ice crystal. Before we were returned to normal size, a simple knowledge had crystallized within me: we are all infinitely unique and immeasurably beautiful. This inherent beauty is constantly unfolding through our unlimited capacity for joy, love, tolerance, and laughter.

Inevitably, we will all encounter difficulties from which we might prefer to shrink; however, those are precisely the moments in which our hearts and minds can expand. And this book will show you how.

How to Make This Book Work for You

This book is a collection of twenty-two stories, and thirty-nine tools. Each one was written with the goal of helping you resolve a difficult situation, improve your mood, or achieve your next great objective.

Each story describes a client's journey to transforming unhappiness into joy, gratitude, and compassion. Along the way, the reader will see representations of lessons learned along the way in the form of tools. Some tools give an organized "how-to" outline for moving forward. Other tools are a visual representation of a helpful framework, designed to present a new perspective for solving difficult issues and questions. In my counseling practice, I've found that representing frameworks visually on a whiteboard makes them easier to remember. Visual learners love them.

Each tool has been tested and retested to make sure it is helpful in everyday life for a wide range of personalities and presenting problems. Each tool has also proven to be a fundamental element in deeper, transformative experiences for clients. The characters and stories in this book represent composites of several individuals and events, as confidentiality is always my top priority. You can read each story for the full experience, or if you want to cut to the chase, you can go straight to the tools.

I've had the privilege of being a counselor and life coach for over twenty years, and this book is the result of watching client after client change his or her life for the better. Everything starts with the first step: being willing to change. My clients have shown me that once you are willing to manifest the courage and vulnerability necessary to share your story, your story will change. These wonderful people are proof that life works when we're dedicated to creating a life that works for us.

Now is the time! Make this book your own. You have an incredible life story waiting to unfold. In this story, your life works for you and allows you to contribute to your family, community, and society.

A Note to Students of Psychology

Imagine it's your first session as a counselor. You open your mouth to greet your client, and instead of "hello," a gasp comes out. Only then do you realize that you've been holding your breath for who knows how long! You'd like to reach out and shake your client's hand, but you're certain the pools of perspiration seeping out of your shirt and down your arms are a dead giveaway of your uncertainty.

The client looks at you with trusting eyes and innocently inquires, "How does this work?" You feel a scream emerging from your throat. "Hell if I know!" you resist yelling. You also resist calling your mother in the middle of the session and begging her to please come get you and take you home.

Somewhere in your mind, you think about dry cleaning. Yes, dry cleaning—where the clothes come in dirty and go out clean, where a spot is a spot and there is no ambiguity. You know you'd be good at dry cleaning; strange that it is only now as this client, this *person*, is staring at you and waiting for answers, that you are able to see so clearly that your answer is a different career.

Your mind, scrambling madly, tries to calm you down: *Just remember the role plays, the videotaped sessions and feedback, and the endless hours transcribing practice sessions.* Your inner cheerleader yells, *You got this!* But when she sees the stricken, nervous look on your face, even she puts down her pom-poms and heads out to look for a new game.

Practice as we might, nothing can prepare us for those first few sessions when we sit across the room from another human being—someone seeking help, relief from suffering, and perspective on how to make a better life.

My first client was desperate. But he wasn't the only one in the room feeling this way. As he shared his story, he began to sweat, and so did I. I sweat in those weird places that activate when your sweating is anxiety based: the upper lip (attractive and not at all distracting) and behind the knees. Worrying about all the perspiration was not at all conducive to that "being present" thing I had just spent three years of graduate school exploring.

Needless to say, it did not go well.

He did not return.

So I sought feedback. "Relax," my mentor said. "You don't have to solve it all at once. Let your client's life story unfold." I thanked her for this advice. Later, I told her that putting three fingers gently over her mouth and chin had failed to conceal the fact that she was laughing at me and my sweating.

After all these years, I'm now in the position of advising psychology students to *relax*! But I know it's harder than that, which is why I wrote this book. Here you'll read about the same concepts that are covered in graduate school but with one big difference: now you'll get to "sit in" on sessions and see how all of those concepts are presented in real time, with real human beings.

Make no mistake—it is important go to class, study the material, and understand the history of psychology and how we got to where we are today. However, this book contains the most crucial lesson that you will not learn in any classroom. I've discovered that truly helping my clients heal can only happen when I bring my authentic self to the counseling room. In the following stories, I'll show you how I am *me* in my sessions so that, should you decide to follow a life dedicated to serving others through psychotherapy and life coaching, you can also learn how to be *you* in the counseling room. Please be reassured that the greatest gift you have to give to your clients is the one you've already been given—your unique presence.

Family Dysfunction in the Life of a Therapist

Believe it or not, psychotherapists and life coaches are not immune to family dysfunction. If anything, we are more aware of it when it inevitably shows up.

That's why I decided to begin this collection with a story from my own family folklore. This is the only story that uses real names and specific individuals. As mentioned previously, the characters in all the other stories represent composites of several people, in order to protect my clients' privacy.

The Road to Success is Dotted with Many Tempting Parking Spots

The four of us are having a great time in the car—considering we are on our way to a funeral. Our laughter comes to a dead stop when we round a corner and see that the church parking lot is full.

"We should have left earlier," my brother says.

"Who would have thought he had so many friends!" remarks my seventy-eight-year-old Aunt Mary. She was never one to worry much about the unintended subtext of her statements.

"I'm not sure how many friends he had, but part of the problem is that the church parking lot is also a park-and-ride for commuters," I observe.

"It's fine," says my ever-optimistic mom. "There's a great spot right over there."

My brother motors the car to the spot. There are disabled-parking-only signs plastered everywhere.

"Ah … this isn't … a good idea," my brother warns.

"It's actually an awful idea!" I add.

"It's fine," Mom repeats, as she deftly pops open the glove box. She slides in her right hand, fishes out a deep-green disabled-parking permit, and loops it onto the rearview mirror, where it swings in happy oblivion.

"Mom!" I scream out in disbelief. "Dad died two years ago! That's expired. And PS: no one in this car is disabled."

"Well, we're certainly glad about that," my aunt responds. She was never one to worry about hijacking a conversation either.

Finally, we park and pile out of the car. I'm grumbling, and my brother is mumbling. We beat feet, since the service begins in five minutes. After songs and speeches, humility and hugs, coffee and cake, we say our goodbyes.

From the steps of the church, we see a man wearing a black vest with the words *Volunteer Police* written in florescent orange. He is transcribing the license plate number of my mother's car onto a long rectangular form. Mom relives her high school track days with a speedy hundred-yard dash to the officer.

Their conversation starts out all right, but when her sweet talk doesn't deter him from his ticket-writing, things go south. The volunteer police officer faces Mom as he rips the ticket off a neat stack of papers in triplicate and unceremoniously flaps it at her. They look alike in a comic book kind of way—each of them with puffed-up chests, pursed that-tasted-sour lips, and spectacularly furrowed eyebrows.

Mom takes the ticket.

We pile back into the car in silence, except for the sounds of seat belts clicking into place. And the hum of the engine. And the rip of the deep-green disabled-parking permit as mom tears it off the rearview mirror.

"Well!" Mom is indignant. She huffs uncharacteristically, "He certainly was a hardnose!"

"Mom, you broke the law!" I say from the safety of the back seat. "It's his job to write you a ticket."

"How can it be a job when *Volunteer* is pasted on your back in neon letters?" my brother wonders aloud.

"Okay, I'm just saying, it's not only Mom; we all knew better before the volunteer confirmed it with a punishment," I respond.

"Well," Mom says again, slightly less indignant, "there is that."

"Whether it's death or tickets, there's no use crying over spilt milk," adds my aunt.

"I believe it's 'spilled' milk," I correct her. And then, unable to stop myself from driving the point home, I continue, "There's no use crying over *spilled* milk."

"Well, la-di-da," replies my aunt, completely carefree.

I look around, thinking maybe I'm in a Woody Allen movie. But no. When I come out of my quick daydream, there's only silence. Then, laughter.

All four of us start belly laughing. Snorting, chortling, giggling, even doing that weird exhale-while-wheezing thing. I love these people—they put the "fun" in family dysfunction. But it's not just family dysfunction or death, tickets, and breaking the law that we're talking about here. It's opportunity. Yes, the opportunity to develop "a humble posture of learning," as my mentor would say.

Later, Mom writes the following letter to City Hall:

> *Dear Most Honorable Judge,*
>
> *I have enclosed the ticket I received and marked the box asking me to explain the circumstances. I realize, however, that there is little to explain. I made a mistake. Yes, I am guilty of an error in judgment and of the behavior that accompanied it. I do ask that my fine be reduced, as I have been driving for over fifty years and have had a perfect record up to this point. I would be very grateful if you could reduce the fine.*
>
> *I am also enclosing half of my deceased husband's disability parking permit. (Did I mention we were married for fifty years and I still miss him every day?)*
>
> *I am keeping the other half to remind myself that the road to success is dotted with many tempting parking spots.*
>
> *Very humbly yours,*
> *Karin*

The most honorable judge deferred the ticket.

"Deferred" is a fancy way of saying that if you've truly understood the error of your ways—which includes deciding to make new, better, healthier, and in this case, legal choices—then we will chalk it up to a learning experience. But if you forget what you've learned or didn't make the effort to humble your ego and pursue change, then we'll give you the ticket and charge you a double fine to boot.

In this case, the most honorable judge seemed to operate a lot like the most honorable universe: encouraging us to recognize that each time we make a decision based on integrity, we manifest our best selves. While attending to the rituals surrounding death, we learned an important lesson about life.

🍴 Tool! The Tyranny of Shortcut, Short-Term Thinking and What to Do About It

How to know when you are pulling into a tempting parking space:

You're in a jam because you should have started earlier or had a better plan but you didn't. Your thinking and decision making probably sounds like this: "Oh well, just this once I'll take the short cut, the easy way out. But only this once, and then next time I'll do better." Maybe this means parking illegally in the disabled-parking spot, or cheating off a friend on a test, or getting high before an important presentation at work. Whatever it may be, we humans are experts at creatively rationalizing and excusing unhealthy or irrational behaviors.

What to do about it:

Stop at once! Do not park the car in the tempting parking space. Instead, pull over so you can make the best long-term decision. These are precisely the situations in which we are given the opportunity to assume a humble posture of learning based not in ego or self-flagellation but in genuine self-reflection.

Ask yourself what part you played in creating this situation. Take an honest look at the role fear has played in making those not-so-optimal choices in the past. More often than not, these patterns are rooted in childhood coping or defense mechanisms. However, as we grow older and gain more control and wisdom, it's important to analyze whether these are still healthy ways of being. This process of self-reflection and self-control may entail unexpected inconveniences, expenses, or discomfort. This is the price we pay for growth. It's better to feel a little discomfort in the moment than wait for fate (otherwise known as the "effect" part of cause and effect) to manifest in a more unpleasant way. Owning up to your part in creating the situation will empower you to stay in the driver's seat of your experiences and make it easier to laugh about later.

Ask yourself what you could do differently in the future. Explore the infinite alternatives available to you. Create your own positive destiny by taking action based in integrity instead of fear or convenience. Then recommit as often as necessary.

Part Two: Counseling Can Be User Friendly

So Many Adventures, So Little Time

Paul is an intelligent, self-identified geek and space enthusiast who works as a software developer. When he comes in for a session with concerns about feeling anxious and overwhelmed with the myriad responsibilities he has both at work and at home, I don't bother doing therapy.

Instead, I tell him a true story.

An astronaut hovers in space, assigned to remove a panel on the Hubble Telescope. He stares at the panel, knowing he must remove thirty screws in as many minutes. To make matters worse, the gloves he's wearing limit his dexterity. Slowly and deliberately he repeats the phrase, "There is only one screw." This intense focus on the present task proves effective in helping him stay solidly in his space boots, instead of jumping around in time. He avoids jumping ahead, where he will become anxious over how much is left to do. He avoids jumping behind to consider similar situations that he has cataloged as failures. He neither retreats into a lost past nor disappears into an imaginary future. *There is only one screw*, he thinks again, removing the screw and securing his success.

When I finish the story, Paul starts filling in the details, including the name of the astronaut and the year of his journey. I thank him for the information yet gently let him know that getting more information about the event wasn't why I told him the story.

"In other words," I say, "anxiety and feeling overwhelmed are also part of your journey. The best way to deal with them is to realize that we can only take action in the moment. When we put 100 percent of our focus in the moment, it naturally helps to rid us of feeling anxious and overwhelmed. If you really want to enjoy the journey through inner space, get engaged with what you're doing in the moment."

Paul grins. "So the moral of the story is: you're screwed if you pay attention to more than one screw."

Clients say the best things.

⚔ Tool! Don't Get Screwed: Live in the Moment

- We can only take action in the present moment.
- Getting and staying focused on the present moment decreases feelings of anxiety and feeling overwhelmed.
- Research confirms that sustained focus on one task beats out multitasking when it comes to efficiency, effort, and results.
- Taking things one step at a time and fully committing to each step of the process are keys to accomplishing each and every goal.

The Call of the Brave

The first voicemail says, "Hi, it's Kelly. Thanks for the ... whaaaat?"

The second voicemail says, "Hi, it's Kelly again. I was checking my mail while I was calling you, and when I saw a letter from you, I panicked and hung up. I thought you might be ditching me because I'm too needy. Now I see it's a pretty card with a nice note thanking me for a referral. What I wanted to say was that our last session was soooooo helpful. And, that said, I'm going to need aaaaaaanother one."

Messages like that make checking my voicemail fun. They also remind me that I can't be of service to a client until they contact me. To make that phone call and leave that voicemail (or goodness forbid, have a conversation if the counselor picks up!) takes the heart of a lion king. To make the call is to courageously admit something is not working.

When a client—especially a new one—calls me, I consider it "The Call of the Brave." Why is it so difficult to make the call? Partly because of lingering social stigmas about people who want to see a therapist. These stigmas assume that you must be

- crazy,
- incapable of managing your life,

- a loser, or
- weak.

It's also difficult to make the call because it requires making yourself deeply vulnerable. However, it is precisely this act of risk taking that allows the healing process to begin. Asking for help represents an act of self-love and ensures that we will have company on our journeys.

Since I never underestimate the amount of courage it takes to pick up the phone, my respect for a client only deepens when he or she actually shows up. Those who do show up quickly feel a sense of relief (one of life's most underrated emotions). Next, life begins to work in mysterious ways to offload the client's troubles while bringing solutions into focus. The benefits of counseling certainly don't end there, but these initial results provide excellent validation of the courage it took to make the call and walk through the door.

Take Kelly's experience. She was in her early thirties and had recently returned to live at home with her mom after a really rotten breakup. She felt unsure of her potential and was toting around a giant question mark regarding her life direction. Through the counseling process, she was able to recognize a variety of self-limiting patterns and beliefs she had unknowingly been repeating. Now she's a managing partner at a legal firm that helps immigrant families through the process of becoming citizens of the United States. She loves her work and new home and also loves helping others create beautiful lives and enjoy living them.

🍴 Tool! Counseling: What It Is and What It Does

- Counseling can provide you with simple yet effective tools to help you feel more hopeful and free and fulfill your greatest potential. One of the most immediate and overlooked benefits of counseling is a feeling of relief.

- Counseling is a place to become aware of your beliefs and to recognize if they are limiting your growth and outcomes in life.
- You don't have to be out-of-your-mind crazy to benefit from counseling. Here are a few reasons why perfectly capable people might decide to seek counseling:
  - They are tired of feeling stuck in an ongoing issue.
  - They want to resolve work or relationship problems.
  - They are dealing with health issues—either their own or those of someone they love.
  - They want support and accountability for accomplishing a big goal.
  - They want to take their lives from "okay" to "fantastic."
- Good counseling includes sharing the latest (relevant) research in the field of psychology with the client.
- The best outcomes occur when you feel safe within the counseling environment and with the counselor.
- Counseling can help you develop the mindset that everything in life is one great experiment in living authentically and enjoying life.

The Ultimate, 100-Percent-Satisfaction-Guaranteed Way to Discover Your Soul Mate

Judy is articulate and precise. She maintains a positive attitude about life—except when talking about "the man issue." Translated from Judy-speak, that means: "There's little hope I'll ever find my soul mate."

Although she came to counseling hoping to deal with "the man issue," she often tries to steer the conversation in other directions. However, because one of her greatest fears is being loved only for her ability to work hard and succeed, we inevitably circle back to it in our conversations—unfortunately with the same deflated sense of futility.

"In the large collection of futile thoughts that clutter my mind, the desire for a soul mate is paramount," she says pithily. Then she adds, "Especially when you consider my ex-husband left me for my best friend."

"That's a giant ouch," I acknowledge. "Still, while it may be futile to resist buying Girl Scout cookies, I don't believe that it's futile for you to want to find a great man to share your life. Maybe there's a more effective way of looking at 'the man issue.'" I choose the word *effective* on purpose, since I know she's hooked on being efficient. I also make a quick mental note that for someone who's exceptionally eloquent, "the man issue" is a pretty lackluster name.

"You just returned from a conference on global warming, right?" I ask.

"Yes, but I didn't find a man there, if that's what you're wondering," she snaps.

"I'm not wondering about that at all," I reply carefully. "I'm just remembering how excited you were to have been chosen to attend. I'm curious if you could describe what you liked so much about the conference."

"Well, I don't know what this has to do with 'the man issue,' but I much prefer discussing the International Conference on Global Warming. Still, I can't tell you what I liked about it," she says flatly. Without smiling, she adds, "I can't tell you what I liked about it ... because I can only tell you what I loved about it!"

I step up to my trusty whiteboard and exclaim, "Perfect!" while writing the heading *Things I Loved about the International Conference on Global Warming* on one half of the whiteboard.

"Start describing," I command.

Judy is thoughtful. She takes a moment, as if considering all the potential options before choosing the best of the best. Finally, she starts talking, and the words pour out; I write feverishly to keep up.

₩◎₽ Tool! What My Soul Mate Really Looks Like: Step One

Things I loved about the International Conference on Global Warming

I was happy to be chosen.

I loved making a contribution.

I loved learning together.

> It felt deeply meaningful to me.
>
> I was so happy to be a participant.
>
> I loved sharing meals with others.
>
> My mind was challenged.
>
> I could be legitimately angry.
>
> My organization chose to fund me 100 percent.
>
> This sounds vain, but I loved the new clothes I wore.

"Excellent!" I enthuse. "Now tell me how you felt at the conference."

Again, Judy is thoughtful. This time, though, she knows immediately. I can see her revel in remembering. Remembering is the bonus pleasure you don't expect.

⑩ Tool! What My Soul Mate Really Looks Like: Step Two

> **How I felt at the International Conference on Global Warming**
>
> I felt happy, free, like it was great to be me.
>
> I liked myself. I felt good about who I was as a person.
>
> I could express myself easily.
>
> I felt immense energy.
>
> I felt excited when I woke up in the morning.

"All of this is great, Judy!" I shout, fully embodying the role of cheerleader. Maybe I'm being a little over the top, but it takes a lot of energy to whip up a crowd of one.

"It certainly reflects happily upon a satisfying time," she concedes.

"The man issue," "the job issue," "the weight issue"—whatever that big, hairy obstacle might be, it all boils down to our fears, expectations, and beliefs. Since Judy has identified a feeling of futility underlying her attitude toward being loved, this is where the shift must occur. Her beliefs about herself are the starting point. Ultimately, it is not about "the man issue" but rather about developing a fundamental belief that she is worthy of love just as she is, simply because she is a walking, breathing human manifestation of love.

"Okay," I say. "I left half of the whiteboard blank so that we could simultaneously address another topic. Let's say the man of your dreams shows up tomorrow. You go on a date and have an incredible time; it is obvious that each of you likes the other. Now, move yourself down the dating road. You're in a longer-term relationship, and you're sure he's your soul mate. Tell me, what does your soul mate expect you be?"

As she starts answering, I jot down her responses in the blank column to the right of the *Things I loved about the Global Warming Conference* column.

¡○¡ Tool! What My Soul Mate Really Looks Like: Step Three

Things I loved about the International Conference on Global Warming	What My Soul Mate Expects Me To Be
I was happy to be chosen.	Pretty
I loved making a contribution.	Sexy
I loved learning together.	Give, give, give
It felt deeply meaningful to me.	Entertaining, funny, interesting 24/7
I was so happy to be a participant.	Undivided attention 24/7
I loved sharing meals with others.	Gourmet chef
My mind was challenged.	Calm, serene, and lovely 24/7
I could be legitimately angry.	Never angry
My organization chose to fund me 100 percent.	Able to support him financially
This sounds vain, but I loved the new clothes I wore.	Somehow be forever young, skinny, and fit

"Excellent!" I enthuse. "Now tell me, how does it make you feel that the person you hoped would add joy to your life expects you to be all these things?" I intentionally choose the words "add joy to your life" instead of "love you unconditionally" because the latter would have cut too deeply, and our wonderful train of thought would have jumped the tracks.

Again, Judy is thoughtful. This time, though, she's certain. I can see her ache in remembering. Remembering is the bitter pain you don't expect.

🍴 Tool! What My Soul Mate Really Looks Like: Step Four

How I felt at the International Conference on Global Warming	How I feel about my soul mate's expectations of me
I felt happy, free, like it was great to be me.	Exhausted
I liked myself. I felt good about who I was as a person.	Resentful
I could express myself easily.	Angry
I felt immense energy.	Defeated
I felt excited when I woke up in the mornings.	Sucks the life out of me

This last task has so exhausted Judy that she's now sitting sideways on the couch with a pillow clutched across her tummy. Her perfect posture has been replaced with a teenage-like slouch. I take this to be a good sign.

"I'm not sure if you're relaxed or exhausted," I comment.

"Me neither," says Judy, shifting the pillow.

"Is it okay if I go on with my theory about why I wanted all of this on the whiteboard?" I ask.

"Go ahead," she says, before adding flatly, "thrill me."

Oh, I'll bring it! I think but don't say aloud, as she is much too well heeled.

Instead, I say, "Here's what I'm thinking: you're a financially independent woman with a successful career and lots of friends, and you want to find your 'soul mate,' to use your words. Yet when we explore your imagined soul mate's expectations of you, they aren't very positive. Take a look at the list. Do you want to be that person? Do you want to have those feelings?"

It's all on the whiteboard, in her own words. The naked truth that comes out when Judy stops compartmentalizing "the man issue."

I cut to the chase. "You want a man who makes you feel like the conference. All the rest is just programming, old beliefs, and assumptions that are no longer useful." I pause before adding, "Your soul mate is Mr. Global Warming!"

"That'd be hot!" she jokes, and the grin looks good on her.

¶⊙¶ Tool! Discover Your Soul mate in Five Easy Steps

1. Identify a cause, hobby, or activity you're passionate about and write down several reasons why you are so drawn to it.

2. Write down how you feel when you're engaged in said cause, hobby, or activity.

3. Write down what you think your ideal soul mate would expect of you and how you'd feel about meeting those expectations.

4. Compare what you have written in steps one and two with what you wrote for step three. Then reflect on the similarities and differences.

5. When looking for a partner, keep envisioning what you've described in steps one and two. When you meet the person who embodies those characteristics, you will have arrived at your soul mate destination. Note: your soul mate doesn't necessarily have to share your interest in the cause, hobby, or activity about which you're passionate—the important part is that being with them brings out your passion and makes you feel wonderful and worthy of love.

5b. If you are feeling unsure, this ol' chestnut of a cliché can actually be quite helpful: does your soul mate make you want to "be a better person"? If not, you might want to reconsider the relationship. If so, celebrate and go become that "better" person!

Shoot for the Stars!

Amy is two years into her teaching career and is already a rising star. She's an honest, intelligent, funny young woman who is loaded with talent and drive. That's why it's so painful to listen to her explain her reasons for quitting her job and giving up on herself.

"No one seems to understand the pressure," she complains at our first session. "I'm answering to so many people about so many things. Six months ago, I might have felt a little anxious by the end of the day. Now I'm anxious from the moment I get out of bed and in a state of panic by the end of class. The only thing that gets me through the day is sheer determination. I demand excellence from myself. I'm completely demanding of everyone else too. It's really horrible." She sobs.

I hear a mixture of relief that her truth is spoken and frustration that this is her truth, but I say nothing.

She peeks out at me from behind the pillow she's put over her face. Was I still there?

"Honestly, though, I'll tell you the real problem. The real problem is that I'm too flawed," she concludes.

"Honestly, though, you're not the first person to believe you're fatally flawed," I reply.

"I didn't say fatally!" she corrects, looking panicked.

"See, you're already ahead of the game! Let me cross out the fatally part from my notes," I joke, while drawing an exaggerated *X* on my notepad.

She laughs and then stops herself, because after all, she's bummed. "Okay, well, I have at least one big flaw, and I just can't do it anymore."

"What is this one big flaw, and what can't you do?"

Amy explains, "I'm flawed because I can't get my kids to the right place. I teach a bilingual kindergarten class. The kids need to be ready for first grade, and they're not. So obviously I'm a flawed teacher. This is my second year in the classroom. And as the year has progressed, I've just gotten more anxious, and we've fallen even more behind. At night and on the weekends, I'm exhausted. But even still, I work all weekend long to try to catch up, you know, to make up for my flaw."

"Flaw-la-la-la-la," I sing to her in my best "Deck the Halls" Christmas-carol voice, even though it's spring.

Her expression is that of Alice falling down the rabbit hole. Despite the fancy furnishings in my office, she has just realized she's landed in Wonderland. She may have a flaw, but she's clearly sitting with the Mad Hatter therapist who is out of touch and out of her mind. Her reaction seems appropriate.

"I know you're feeling terrible, so maybe that was a terrible thing to do—especially given my vocal abilities. But I wanted you to know what I think about 'fatally flawed' human beings: they don't exist. What do exist are imperfect people who are wonderful and lovable just as they are," I explain.

She glares at me. This is common when I suggest to perfectionists that it is okay to be messy or imperfect. I decide to leave that one alone for the moment and continue, "What also exists is our terror that we won't be able to live up to other people's expectations. And what makes it worse is the fear that we won't be loved or be able to love ourselves if we fail to be perfect."

"But I *am* failing, and I won't be able to live up to their expectations! How come everyone keeps trying to console me? Why won't you just let me be flawed?" she asks exasperatedly.

"Because calling yourself flawed is passing a harsh judgment on yourself. I can't make you change your beliefs—you are welcome to decide you're flawed and that it's your story and you're stickin' to it. But ethically, I have to challenge your beliefs if they're working against you and making you suffer. For instance, right now, because you believe you're flawed, you're stuck with this cruel self-judgment and criticism as a way of life. Just like it's your job to teach children, it's my job to teach you kinder ways of treating yourself."

"That *sounds* nice," she responds curtly. "But you're ignoring two things: First, I'm already doing poorly, and if I'm nice to myself, then things will certainly go to hell in a hand basket, as my Grandmother used to say. And second, the truth is, I just can't live up to the expectations for me." She declares this, confident in her incompetence.

Why is it, I wonder, that when I challenge clients to think more kindly of themselves, they immediately believe that things will go to hell in a hand basket if they do? I've concluded that most of us have spent so much time pushing ourselves through our daily to-do lists with a mixture of distrust and disdain that we've learned to attribute our successes to rigid and unrelentingly cruel self-talk.

My mind floats away for a moment, and I'm standing in a well-worn dance studio in a bad part of San Francisco. The dance teacher at the front of the room has tons of performance credentials and lots of pull in the professional community, and she mentors many of the biggest rising stars in the area. I want to shoot for the stars, so here I am in her class every night.

She's "old school" in her belief that degrading her students is the way to help us rise. Some dancers respond well to this treatment, but I mostly feel anxious and perform well below my capabilities. One night, I'm not alone in under-performing. Everyone is displeasing her. So she takes the LP off the record player (I told you she was old school) and flings it through the air like a thin, grooved Frisbee while screaming at us about our ineptitude.

I'd heard legendary stories about the LP Frisbee. What I am so surprised to witness that night is the response from the students: they simply duck as a dangerous piece of plastic with momentous torque flies just past their heads! As if this was the most normal way for a mentor to treat her mentees. I finish the class and vow never to return. I decide from then on to stay away from anyone who would try to punish me into becoming perfect.

As my daydream ends, I address Amy. "Okay, since I know you won't take my word for it, would you be willing to do an experiment? Try speaking kindly to yourself for one week. Let yourself off the hook when things aren't prefect—when you're not being a perfect teacher, when your students aren't acting like perfect students, and so on. If you find that things 'go to hell in a hand basket,' then you can certainly return to beating yourself up."

"Okay, I'll try it," she says begrudgingly.

"Good. Now, you've said this several times, so I really want to understand it. What can't you live up to?" I ask.

I'm awestruck at her response. She's in her second year as a kindergarten teacher in a bilingual public school and is in charge all by herself of twenty-eight five-year-olds, many of whom are emotionally and developmentally young for their age. In addition, she's required to get every student up to first-grade level to graduate, which means achieving the following standards—some of which seem daunting even for a fifty-year-old—in just nine months:

- Carry out social interactions in a foreign environment.
- Read and write at an advanced grade level.
- Follow directions and learn new protocols while simultaneously developing emotionally, intellectually, and artistically.
- Be able to spend a full day learning in either of two languages.

Because Amy could not get all of twenty-eight five-year-old students to achieve these standards in less than nine months, she "knew" she was flawed. When she senses that I think the bar is set just a *little* too high, she points out Ms. Sheila's classroom, where "the angels seem to sing and the children are always fully attentive." What she doesn't initially mention is that Ms. Sheila has been teaching for twenty years. In fact, Ms. Sheila was the one who asked the school principal to give Amy extra support and convince her not to quit—Ms. Sheila knew that the learning curve was steep for new teachers and didn't want an excellent educator to fall by the wayside.

It's thanks to the school principal that Amy is in therapy. Amy says, "If I do this counseling thing, then I can quit teaching fair and square." But nothing about her situation is fair or square. She has an abundance of high-need kids in an exceptionally challenging environment. Amy was trying to shove each kid into a set model of accomplishment that wasn't realistic. After months of this, she had become riddled with anxiety and saw their failures as a reflection of her own ineptitude. So she began punishing herself with thoughts like

I'm flawed;
I'm a terrible teacher;
I can't handle the stress;
I'm not smart or talented enough; and
They deserve a better teacher than me.

"Wow," I respond. "You know, if you spoke to your students that way, you'd be charged with child abuse."

Amy looks surprised. This was the first thing I'd said that really got her attention, so I break it down: because she was freaked out about being flawed, her students had become mirrors and reflected that belief back to her. They reacted by manifesting their own five-year-old version of being flawed and freaked-out. Simply put, the more punishment Amy inflicted on herself, the more her students acted out. When her stress and anxiety had reached their apex a few days earlier, one eager-to-please student had walked up to her desk—presumably to ask a question—and burst into tears.

When they weren't crying, the students made comments that revealed how deeply they had internalized the ambiance of defeatism:

"I'm bad, even though I try to be good. So I'm no good."

"I'm a bad student."

"I hate this class."

"I can't do it! I can't do anything!"

"I'm not as good as her, so you like her better than me."

Once we make this connection, Amy immediately shifts her attitude. "I don't ever want them to feel that way!" she exclaims.

"I know. So quit punishing yourself," I respond.

"What do I do instead?" she asks.

Such a great question.

Over the next few weeks I teach her the "Practice Not Punishment" process. I tell her that when external demands become overwhelming, as they often do—especially for high performers who are always shooting for the stars—instead of falling into self-flagellation, she should try to practice toward her goals.

Amy uses this idea to realistically examine where her kids are in their development. But instead of coming from a place of frustration about her abilities, or theirs, she finds creative new ways to practice toward the target goals. When it takes her students five minutes to form a straight line for recess, though the guideline for graduating into first grade is that "students can form a line in less than one minute," she no longer gets upset. She simply praises the students for trying to make the line and tells them they will keep practicing this skill. She also explains why it's important to learn how to line up quickly (so they can each have a buddy, make sure no one is missing, and get the most time for recess). Two days later, all twenty-eight kids can line up lickety-split.

Every time a student falls behind or acts out, Amy simply says, "It's okay. We'll just do a little more practicing." When it comes time for the end-of-the-year museum field trip, her twenty-eight five-year-olds listen to instructions brilliantly, and everyone has a great time. Amy proudly reports, "The museum docent said that in fifteen years he's never seen so many little ones listen so well. He told me, You've done good work. I told him, We just practice a lot."

And with all that practice comes a lot of love. The students start telling her, "I love you Ms. Amy!" and "You're the best teacher!"

"I'm a more happy and relaxed teacher too!" Amy reports. "Next year, we're going to start practicing from day one."

I nod. Next year, when Amy the rising star will keep shooting for them.

⅋◯⅃ Tool! How to Use the "Practice Not Punishment" Process

Part One:

- Shoot for the stars! That is, aim high and set big goals.
- Stand proudly right where you are and break down into small steps what you need to do to reach each goal.
- Pick a goal and start practicing consistently until you excel at the first step.
- Then practice the second step consistently until you excel at that too.
- Celebrate your efforts and successes (no matter how small!) along the way until you achieve your goal!

Part Two:

- When you aren't performing at the level you'd like to be, let go of judgment and negative self-talk. Do not engage in harsh or relentless self-criticism.
- Recommit to practicing toward your goal.

From Perpetual Worrier
to Peaceful Warrior

I walk into the waiting room and call her name. First sessions always remind me of going on a blind date—wandering into a room full of strangers and wondering *Which one is mine?* She stands up, and I consciously work to keep my jaw from dropping. I have had many good-looking clients, but she isn't one of them.

Candace is drop-dead gorgeous. She is tall and blonde with bright blue eyes and curves that must elicit endless catcalls.

Ten minutes later, she tells me she's the plaintiff in a workplace-sexual-assault lawsuit. Then, self-consciously, she starts to cry. The sense of genuine goodness that oozes from her almost makes me feel sorry for the guy who harassed her, only because I suspect he's going to fry in front of the jury. But by the time I hear the third of seventy-two instances of sexual harassment she's suffered—including but not limited to repeated sexually explicit comments about her body made in front of her coworkers—I'm ready for him to feel the heat and "pony up," to use an expression often repeated by her attorney to refer to paying (in dollars) for his deeds.

But Candace isn't concerned about the money. She's concerned that the law doesn't mandate rehabilitation to guarantee that he will learn how to treat women with respect. She says, "It's infuriating that my only option for seeking justice and making sure this doesn't happen to another woman is to go after his money."

Besides her good looks, Candace has been graced with a big heart. After just one session, I can see that her real problem is that she's too nice to the wrong people. And, well, she's paranoid.

Because she had to tolerate and make nice with people at work who were treating her badly, she started directing all of her frustration toward her family and became a "disgruntled evil bitch" (her words!) at home. In addition, the more she was mistreated, the more her brain began concocting crazy conspiracy theories.

"I can't get out of the driveway without feeling panicked now," she confesses. "Once the garage door opens, I fear for my children and myself. I'm afraid that the perpetrator will be outside my home and he'll shoot me. Or that he'll jump into my car, take my children, and hold them hostage until I drop the lawsuit. I think I sound crazy. Do you think so? Do you think I sound crazy?"

I pause for a moment and do my best to look profoundly thoughtful while sliding my glasses down my nose to peer at her. "Yes," I reply.

Her blue eyes widen.

"Yes," I repeat, "you're starting to sound a little crazy. But my guess is that your thinking is trauma related, so I don't see any straightjackets in your future. However, I do have a tool I think you might find helpful."

While I sound calm, my fingers are twitching with anticipation. I can feel the blue marker in my hand and imagine gliding it smoothly across the whiteboard. I'd start with blue and then add in lavender, because lavender is always good for this drawing. Alas, the drawing must wait. You can't dive deep when the surface waters are windswept with post-traumatic stress, especially when the trauma is showing up as paranoia.

"This tool is based on the fact that no matter what we're told, we tend to trust our own lived experiences most of all," I continue. "There are two parts to this tool. The first part is about rebuilding your confidence that you are safe. When people have been traumatized, one of the natural responses is to get a little loopy from overthinking all the potential bad things that could happen in the future. They start to imagine that some terrible surprise is lurking behind every bush, hiding in every nook or cranny. Since the brain evolved to help us survive, that survival instinct gets turned up to eleven (Candace snort-laughs, so I know she gets the Spinal Tap reference).

I continue explaining. "There isn't a lot of use in trying to dismiss these fears as mere 'crazy thinking' because the person won't believe it. And that will make him or her feel even more 'crazy'. But we can question the fears, as well as the strange visions they cause and the panic they bring to the surface. So the tool I recommend is very simple: every time you're afraid, stop and ask yourself, 'Am I okay now? Am I safe now? Are my children safe now?'"

"I usually am safe! And so are my kids!" Candace bursts out with the excitement of understanding. However, she immediately follows up her enthusiasm with the practiced apologizing of a perennial people-pleaser. "I'm so sorry I cut you off. I didn't mean to interrupt you."

We don't know one another too well yet, but my fondness for her is growing faster than the weeds in my garden. And that's saying something.

"Candace," I say deliberately, "this is your time. You can interrupt me whenever you feel like it. Just so you know, though, I didn't feel cut off. I felt like you were being genuinely enthusiastic." She tears up a bit again and then apologizes. And then apologizes for apologizing.

I tell her part of this process is learning to recognize when you do and don't really need to apologize. Another part of this process is to recognize rotten treatment and not put up with it. I congratulate her for summoning up the courage to walk down the path of justice, even when it flattens her with migraines.

Three months later, her paranoia is under control. She tells me, "The 'Am I okay now? Am I safe now?' thing really works! At first, I was asking myself seventeen times a minute if I was safe, if my kids were safe. One day my son even told me, 'Mom, I've called your name five times!' And I hadn't heard him because I was too busy asking myself if we were safe. I don't know when things changed, but yesterday it occurred to me that I don't have those disturbing thoughts anymore. I'm not always waiting for something bad to happen!"

Now it's time to move on to the second tool. I'm still yearning to swim in deeper waters, but I know we are getting there. As much patience as I need, Candace needs three times that of courage. And she continually manifests it. She moves powerfully through her days, fulfilling her responsibilities as a full-time employee, mother of three young kids, and loving wife.

"I'm not so sure about the loving part," she admits. "I'm so stressed out, and after smiling at people all day, I tend to take it out on my husband. I'm too short with the kids too. It's not just my career and the workload, it's how I approach everything; I can't stop worrying."

It's true. She's made great headway in her legal case, yet she's worried the perpetrator will sneak out of the country. She was named the top-performing employee of the year and was asked to be on a distinguished panel of advisors for her company, but she worries about displeasing her boss. Both she and her husband are earning more money than they ever have, but she's constantly worrying about their finances. Her kids are happy and healthy, and she has a great circle of friends. She's only missing one thing: the ability to enjoy it.

"Okay," I say. "Since you've mastered the first tool, let's move on to the second tool. Anytime you're feeling consumed with worry, ask yourself, 'What can I do about it?' If there is something you can do about it, do it. If not, go have fun."

"Now you're really starting to sound crazy," she says skeptically.

"Fair enough," I admit. I know I have to elaborate, so I tell her a story about being a first-time homeowner. When I was only three months into owning my first house, I woke up one sunny Saturday morning filled with vim and vigor. I pranced out to my mailbox, and the next thing I knew, I was reading a threatening letter from my mortgage company saying I that I was behind in my payments and that they might pull my mortgage! Obviously, I panicked. First, I called my trustworthy real estate agent, and she assured me it's nothing, merely a form letter sent automatically by some computer. My payment probably just got mixed up in the mail.

She was so reassuring that after I hang up with her, I felt fine for about three minutes. Then my panic set in again. This time I called my trustworthy brother. He also assured me it was nothing, just a form letter sent automatically by some computer. My payment probably just got mixed up in the mail. I hung up and felt good for another three minutes.

Then, I began to worry again. I couldn't let it go. *What should I do?* I asked myself. I could call more people, but that didn't seem to help. I couldn't call the mortgage company until Monday morning at nine o'clock, which was exactly forty-eight hours and two minutes from then. So what could I do? I challenged myself to think of any possible action to take.

"Then all of a sudden, I had a flash of brilliance!" I state ceremoniously.

"If you do say so yourself!" she quips. I like very much that she's becoming "impolite" enough to cut me off without so much as an "I'm sorry."

"Indeed!" I laugh. "What I suddenly realized was this: I loved this home, and if they were going to take it away from me on Monday, then I'd better enjoy every second of it this weekend! I'd been so busy that I had forgotten about the newly redecorated deck that overlooked a grove of gorgeous trees and a gentle stream. I cancelled all my plans for the weekend and dedicated myself to completely enjoying some much-needed restorative time. Forty-eight hours later, when I called the mortgage company, I was rested and cheery. The mortgage represetative tells me, 'I don't know why you received that letter. All of your payments have been received on time.'"

By challenging myself to think about what action I could take to solve my problem, my brain kicked into gear and came up with a great idea—and I actually had a better weekend because of the letter. If I'd let myself just worry about it, though, I would have been on the phone obsessively all weekend—which means I would've reached Monday exhausted and then dragged all week long. This tool is simple and straightforward: our brains will kick it up a notch if we replace worry with a call to action.

Three months later, Candace's worry is under control. "That 'What can I do about it?' thing really works!" she says. "At first, it was super hard to use. You know, simple doesn't mean easy! But I just kept practicing it because I knew that's what you'd say: 'Keep practicing the tool.' Then I got it! I figured out how to challenge myself instead of worrying, and my brain kicked into gear!"

I'm so happy for her, yet I feel a wave of nervousness. After six months of waiting, it's finally time to draw on the whiteboard. I don't know why I feel so hesitant about it when I know it's the logical next step. She's doing so great. But I don't want to lose her, because after learning all those practical tools, we are finally going to get a little philosophical.

I breathe in deeply.

"I'm going to draw you a picture," I begin, picking up the blue marker. "Bear with me, because I'm going to draw and explain everything but it might take a minute to see where I'm going with all of this. Okay?"

Candace looks unsure. I can feel my facial muscles contorting into the "trust me I'm a professional" look, attempting to convince her.

"Okay, let's go," she slurs, the words coming out in super-quick succession. This is what it means to be courageous.

"Awesome!" I say, suddenly getting charged up. I feel like a racehorse at the starting gate when the metal barrier between me and the racetrack is lifted.

🍴 Tool! The Mental Triangle

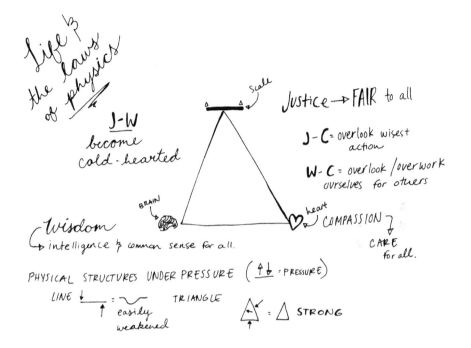

First, I draw a line and start explaining that one line by itself isn't very strong; any pressure on the line will compromise it. But if you connect two more lines, you can build a triangle. Triangles are very stable and can withstand lots of pressure—at this moment I try not to notice how confused she looks.

I tell her that this triangle represents our mental health, and name the three points: wisdom, compassion, and justice. If we are missing any of the points, then we are left with only two lines, which represent a weak and unstable life state. For instance, if we only have wisdom and compassion, we may overwork ourselves in an effort to help others and risk being taken advantage of. If we only have compassion and justice, we may lack the wisdom to discern the best courses of action. And if we only have justice and wisdom, we may become arrogant and cold-hearted. When we create a triangle by connecting all three points, we create a strong mental and emotional state of life that allows us to withstand life's vicissitudes and choose the most effective courses of action.

I pause to check in with Candace, thinking ahead to examples I could use from our previous sessions to clarify each point. But I notice a couple of tears are sliding down her cheeks. She's gotten the point.

"That's spot on," she affirms quietly.

Another month goes by. Candace tells me, "I can't stop thinking about that triangle. It's really effected my perspective on things. It even helped me decide to end a long-time friendship. The only reason I've stayed friends with this girl is because we've known one another since we were children. But she's always been a gossip, and I found out that she's gone behind my back numerous times and made fun of things that I told her in confidence. I shouldn't have been surprised, but she sure was when I said I was done."

She continues, "Then last week when a male stranger said, 'Look at your calves! You've got the biggest calves I've ever seen,' I didn't just take it and smile and hate him. I said, 'Does your mother know you run around town harassing women about their bodies?' The look on his face gave me a good laugh, and then I just forgot about him."

She keeps going, getting more and more excited. "Next I decided we could be saving more money, so I trimmed four hundred dollars off our monthly budget, starting with the two pints of ice cream that my husband and I eat while watching TV after the kids go to bed. I told him I had better uses for the money and the time. Our intimate life is hot again. Plus, after cutting out the ice cream, we're both losing weight. I decided to take advantage of that and start working out too. So now I get to see another mom-friend three times a week, and we're both doing regular workouts and getting strong!"

Unfortunately, this positivity disappears when she tells me her lousy lawyer has taken the liberty of proposing a settlement fee without informing her. Still, Candace agrees it's the best option. Her relief is palpable as she tells me, "After three years of fighting, the end is in sight." Her lawyer announces the payoff date and then misses it and doesn't tell her. Finally he resets the payoff date and then misses it again. He doesn't tell her and stops responding to Candace's calls.

"I bet he's going under and she's taken the money ..." Candace is frantic. "Do you think he's leaving the country? He is, right?"

For a second, I think, *Right back to square one.* But I know better; it's the final push.

"What do you mean a 'final push'?" Candace's voice is high pitched and irritated.

"Like in the adventure movies, right before the hero wins the day! She has to face a personal demon," I explain. Immediately, I see she is in no mood for the wanderings of my mind. "Okay," I say, knowing that's the unspoken-but-agreed-upon word she and I use when we get down to business. "Here's the deal. Your lawyer isn't communicating with you, and you're just accepting it. Because you're accepting it, you're going back to the old school days of paranoia and worry. But that's okay, because we all backslide now and then."

I pull out my stern voice, the one I discovered during tech week while directing two hundred kids in a musical theatre production. "But here's what you're going to do. You're going to act like the strong lady you've become. You're going to use your well-polished politeness to politely tell your lame-acting lawyer that you are done. You are going to lay out your expectation that he will get you the money by the end of the day."

"He's already left her office for today," Candace responds, sounding dejected and uncertain.

"Then call him up tomorrow morning," I coach. "I want you to use the words *done* and *today.*" Then I lay out the final bit. "Right now you're a victim to your lawyer. Lay the victim role to rest. I know you can do it."

"I don't know," she answers.

After months of progress, the end of this session is definitely a downer. But the next day, she calls me.

"It's done! I was firm, and I did it." I can hear the triumph in her voice. The next time I see her, she is radiant.

"It's really done! I fought the fight, and now I can move on with my life. My great life! That's what I've learned, that I have a great life. I get a little money out of the deal, but when the lawyer gets his take and I repay my savings for monies I put out, well, it's certainly not about making a profit. It's okay though. I truly want to move on."

Her life has outgrown the lawsuit.

She's so happy. She continues, "Plus I got a chance to patch things up with a few family members. I still feel stressed around my mother, but when I was with the rest of my family recently, I enjoyed every minute. It used to feel like pressure, but now it feels like joy. Same with my friends; I used to feel pressure in social situations, and now I genuinely enjoy it."

She pauses, waiting for me to say something.

"I'm going to have to give you my insurance card so you can bill me for this session," I say.

She laughs but then gives me that spellbindingly blue-eyed serious look of hers. "You've really helped me get here."

I smile at her while wondering, what it is with our sessions? Is it her tremendous heart? Her constant courage in the face of small and large obstacles? I feel like I want to cry.

She's crying a bit but dabs at her eyes and makes sure to let me know they are happy tears. That's the politest thing she's done in months, and it fits the situation.

"This is the biggest cheeseball statement ever, but I've gone from being the angry bitch that smiles all day and then takes my anger home to sincerely loving life. I was so anxious about life before, but now I just feel appreciation. My husband told me it was so wonderful to hear my laugh echo around the house again. I didn't even realize I'd stopped laughing. And now that I'm laughing and not yelling, my kids are quieter, and they can't get enough of me. My friends even tell me I'm inspiring them to become more loving."

She declares, "I'm getting to know me, and I don't want to waste another minute complaining. I want to see the opportunities for connection and love that exist everywhere. See, I am crazy."

"Yes," I reaffirm. "You're crazy in the best, most wonderful way possible."

There is something else that is wonderful from my point of view. I try to describe it. "We know from reliable sources that the perpetrator's life is the same or worse than before the lawsuit, while yours is so much better. There are many definitions of *Karma*, but in this case I think it means that the closest he'll ever get to love is sneaking sexual harassment, whereas you get to live a rich life filled with love and meaningful connection."

We're both quiet a moment. Some days I simply cannot believe I am paid to have these kinds of conversations. Other days, I earn every penny. Yet life-to-life connection is ultimately priceless.

Candace speaks softly and with great care, once again allowing me to see the thoughtful, serious side of this fun-loving bombshell. "I can't imagine that I'd lived my whole life being that small person. I smiled for everyone without knowing who I was. I have a lot more to sort through, but everything has transformed. Instead of worrying, I think about putting love out in the world. I'm one big ball of love! One big cheeseball of love!"

She's also one big smile as she says this.

"Fantastic!" I enthuse. Then I wonder aloud, "I can't imagine what's next."

"Okay," she says. She pauses dramatically and then nails me with a serious look. "What's next is learning to love my crazy mother."

At that, we both laugh until we cry.

⑂◯⑃ Tool! "Am I Okay Now?": Cure Irrational Fears with One Simple Question

Acknowledge your feelings of fear or apprehension, and then ask yourself, "Am I okay now?" Your answer will usually be yes.

As you repeatedly use this tool, your mind will start connecting fears and apprehensions to the knowledge that nothing bad is actually happening in that moment. You are okay, and you are safe. Over time, this will allow you to release the feelings of fear and apprehension.

⫯◯⫯ Tool! "What Can I Do Now?": Cure Persistent Worry with One Simple Question

When worry creeps into your thinking, ask yourself, "What Can I Do Now?" If there is something you can do in that moment, do it. If there isn't something to be done, go do something fun. This encourages your mind to creatively problem-solve and also teaches you how to let go of things you can't control.

⫯◯⫯ Tool! The Mental Triangle Review

- Remember: good mental health follows the laws of physics and nature. A line is weak, but a triangle can withstand heavy pressure. Make choices based on the triangle of compassion, wisdom, and justice.
- Human beings grow through simple acts. Be kind. Be wise. Be fair. Stand up for what is right. Seize the day.

The End of the Should Story

My counseling sessions are rarely exhausting—with one reliable exception. It's exhausting to listen to the litany of things my clients "should" do. For instance: Melody should lose twenty pounds. Travis should be on time for meetings. Rachel should take the long dreamed of European vacation. Tom should have more fun. Blake should give up law and become a stage actor. Martha should walk the dog more often. Sam should live in the present moment, something he's been "planning" to do for a long time.

Blah, blah, blah.

Should implies we aren't enough just as we are, which is a terrible starting point for any endeavor. Additionally, *should* implies we'll probably never reach our goals because there is always something more we should be doing. That creates a deflating catch-22; no matter what actions we take, even with the very best of intentions and despite giving our whole selves, if we act based on "should," we lose the chance to experience true joy because we're responding to a mandatory impulse rather than an authentic one.

But there is a way out of this vicious cycle. Instead of droning on about what you "should" do, try imagining what you "could" do; this simple change in language turns dull and exhausting into bright and exhilarating. For instance, if Melody wanted to, she could lose twenty pounds. If Travis wanted to, he could be on time for meetings. If Rachel wanted to, she could take the long-dreamed-of European vacation. If Tom wanted to, he could have more fun. If Blake wanted to, he could give up law and become a stage actor. If Martha wanted to, she could walk the dog more often. If Sam wanted to, he could live in the present moment.

Could denotes choice. Like a good friend, *could* offers us encouragement, enthusiasm, and hope, which energizes our body, mind, and spirit. And it actually gets better. Ultimately, *could* allows us to embrace possibility. *Could* says that even what seems impossible might just work.

W. H. Murray, an impressive mountaineer, put it more elegantly: "I have learned a deep respect for one of Goethe's couplets: 'Whatever you can do or dream you can do, begin it. Boldness has genius, power, and magic in it. Begin it now!'"

Now is the time to lose twenty pounds, be on time for meetings, take the long-awaited European vacation, have more fun, follow your creative impulses, walk the dog, and live in the present moment. Now is the time to determine the authenticity of your goal. Is your goal something you feel is truly important? Or does it have the quality of belonging to someone else (thanks Mom and Dad, but this one is mine!). Decide what you really want to accomplish and make now the time to make all of your "coulds" come true.

🍴 Tool! Two Simply Profound Questions to Open Up Your Unlimited Potential

Write out the answers to the following questions:

1. What should you do? Why should you do it?

2. Rewrite or rethink your answers in terms of "could." What, if you wanted to, could you do? Why aren't you doing it?

2b. If the answer you wrote for number two is "I don't really want that," then listen. If the answer is "I'm afraid," then find someone to help you through that fear. If the answer is "I'd really like to do that; it's who I am," then focus your whole heart, resources, and energy on living and enjoying living who you are.

Part Three: Counseling Can Help You Make Important Decisions

The Unknown is Faithful

Suzanne is the first and only client I've ever had who pet her homework assignment. I know I'll have to point it out eventually, since body language and gestures play a significant role in the therapeutic process, but I want to savor the sweetness of the moment. It's like watching a mother reassure a frightened child by gently stroking the child's hair.

"Do you realize you're petting your homework?" I ask her, trying to sound as nonchalant as possible.

"I'm what?" she asks.

"You're petting your homework," I note casually.

"Oh. I guess I am," she acknowledges, sounding equally unconcerned.

"What's on your homework that's bringing out so much affection?" I ask.

Suzanne's homework assignment was to take a plain piece of notebook paper and fold it in half lengthwise. On one side of the piece of paper, I asked her to write the heading "What I want for myself." On the other side, I asked her to write the heading "What others want from me." She was petting the "What I want for myself" side.

This homework assignment was my response to a question Suzanne asked me within minutes of our initial meeting: "Should

I leave my husband after twenty-nine years of marriage?" She explained that she had never sought counseling before, but knew she needed help with this very big question. We both knew that I couldn't give her the answer, but I could help her discover a solid solution.

I suggested that a good place to start would to look at where she wanted her life to go and how well that matched up with where she was now. "In order to get the most out of this homework assignment," I had said, "it's important to keep the paper folded so you can only see the list you're writing, not both lists at the same time."

She stops petting her list and admits, "I really liked this assignment—obviously." She hesitates, inhaling then exhaling deeply. "I'll just show it to you, because you'll see it is really eye-opening" And she hands me the folded paper.

I unfold it.

She's right. My eyes open wide as I read through and compare the two lists.

ⵜ◯ⵜ Tool! What I Want for Myself and What Others Want from Me

What I want for myself	What others want from me
Trust	Loyal
Laughter	Dependable
Joy	Good listener
Travel	Problem solver
Love	Love
Sensuality	Duty
New experiences	Responsible
Connection	Rock to lean on
Optimistic outlook	Steady attitude
To stretch creatively	Hardworking

"Wow, each side is significantly different, yet love is aligned on both! That's beautiful," I remark.

"Well, I followed your instructions to look at only one side at a time. So I was really surprised when I unfolded the page. The last thing I expected to see was *love* written on the same line on both sides. But everything else was ... kinda different." She pauses to reflect, "I like being the person that others expect me to be, but right now it feels like it's at my expense, not my expanse. Being that person for others all the time isn't helping me grow. Still, seeing *love* written gave me hope, especially because my emotions are all over the place and I feel so stuck."

Suzanne is having huge emotional swings, something new and disturbing for this usually cool-as-a-cucumber creative thinker. She tells me that since she began seriously considering divorce, she's been "so angry" one minute and "so sad" the next. Or "so sure" one day and "so hesitant" the next.

"Ah," I recognize. "I have a tool—a framework really—for talking about that. I call it the Emotional Pendulum."

"I don't know what that means yet, but it sounds about right," she jokes.

🍴 Tool! The Emotional Pendulum

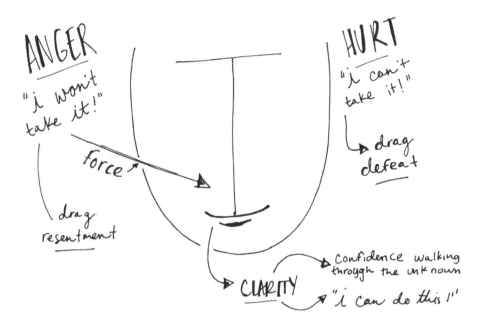

I laugh and then draw and explain. Let's just say the results of me doing more than one of those things at the same time are in, and our survey clearly shows that multitasking can take a hike. But is it right for Suzanne to take a hike?

I launch into my speech. "I like to think about physical structures and properties, since we exist in the physical world. So I use this pendulum to represent our emotions. When a pendulum is at rest, it hangs near the center. This center point is called the equilibrium position. But if you apply force to the pendulum, it will begin to swing. The amount of swing is determined by the amount of force. You can see this illustrated in the drawing with the arrow."

Turning away from the whiteboard to look at Suzanne, I say, "In your case, the force has been brewing over the last many years and is now exploding with energy. Asking and answering the question 'Should I stay or should I go?' exerts a huge force on your emotional pendulum. This causes your emotional pendulum to swing wildly from one side to the other. For most of us, when our pendulum hits a high point of sadness and hurt, we think frantically, *This is it! I can't take it anymore.* But then it swings in the other direction, gathering a ferocious momentum that takes it right past the equilibrium position to the top of the other edge of the emotional pendulum. Here's the high point of anger and frustration where we adamantly declare, 'No, this is it! I won't take it anymore.'"

Seeing Suzanne nod in understanding, I continue. "Humans do not like experiencing intense sadness or anger, so it's only natural that we would want to make a decision when the pendulum is at its highest in order to escape those extreme feelings. If we make a decision from a place of sadness, we might feel better in the moment, but when we try to move forward, most people will find they are dragging a heavy load of baggage that says, 'I got defeated in life.' Suddenly, moving forward is much more difficult because so much energy is spent lugging around this sense of defeat.

"In a similar way, if we make a decision from a place of anger, we'll probably feel relieved in the moment, but when we try to move forward, most people will discover they are dragging a heavy load of baggage that says, 'I got ripped off by life.' And as you might suspect, hauling around all that resentment requires a lot of energy."

Moving my hand along the curve on the whiteboard, I close in on the finish. "As long as the pendulum is making broad swings, we are simply reacting to life, not taking conscious action on our own terms. We want to escape our emotional anguish, yet if we make a decision based in anger, we have to live with the resulting resentment. And if we make a decision based in sadness, we have to live with the resulting hurt and disappointment.

"Instead, we need to ride it out. Our biggest task is deciding to wait for the emotional pendulum to gently rock to-and-fro until it reaches the equilibrium position. At this point, something wonderful happens. As your emotional pendulum settles, you find emotional balance and mental clarity. When that happens, you'll know deep inside what the right decision is, and even if it is difficult, the clarity will see you through."

"I was with you for the anger and hurt," Suzanne says, "but you kinda lost me with the clarity. How can you be so sure it will arrive?"

"Perfectly healthy skepticism!" I say. "I wish I could give you a scientific answer based in research. I do keep up with the latest research, but honestly, this knowledge is based on my lived experience of watching clients make important decisions for over twenty years. The people who wait for clarity always find it, and the wait always serves them well."

"Sounds good, but I'm still not sure I believe you," she replies.

"There's no reason you should believe me," I respond. "Yet hopefully I've proven trustworthy enough for us to keep working together."

"Well, I really liked the homework assignment, so I think I can extend a little trust on the clarity part," she says amicably.

"Awesome," I say. "Now just watch carefully to see what unfolds in your life—because though I might have nice words, what will really convince you is your own lived experience."

We pause. I realize I haven't addressed the "feeling stuck" part of her concern. I think for a minute, and then it comes to me.

Gently, I lay out a theory. "I believe that when we feel stuck it means we're afraid to let go of the outcomes of our decisions. We often want to control not only what the outcomes will be but also other people's perceptions of our decisions. But the outcomes are unknowable and impossible to control. However, when we make decisions while standing firmly in our truths, then no matter what the outcomes, we will experience freedom and vitality."

"I know what I'm going to do," Suzanne says suddenly.

Though I don't know what she is going to say, I can see that she has raced by me and has already taken our conversation to the next level in her thinking. Her long figure lengthens as she shifts positions on the couch.

"I'm going to ask for a separation. Then I'm going to wait for a year before making a decision. I'll live through each season, each holiday, each birthday, and our thirtieth wedding anniversary, and I'll pay attention to the emotional pendulum."

"Remember: when the emotional pendulum hits the equilibrium point, you'll know your truth," I say, wondering if I sound like a Disney fairy godmother. "Then, even if it's hard, it will somehow be easy because you'll have found clarity."

But what happened next was anything but easy. Suzanne's husband begrudgingly moved into an apartment. The only people more upset than him were their children, her siblings, and the entire extended family. Except her dad. He seemed to understand, and he stood by her, trusting her wholeheartedly.

Her friends and employees wondered what was up, first commenting on her reddish, puffy eyes and then noticing that she had a new radiance and was losing weight. Suzanne said, "The weight just seemed to fall off as the heaviness of making this decision lifted off my heart."

She began following her heart, though that meant going into the unknown. She admitted, "It's scary, but it's working out each time."

Indeed! Suzanne was meeting new friends, enjoying a variety of social activities, and taking up old hobbies, like tennis, and new ones, like scuba diving. She expanded her business in a time of economic insecurity and gained creative and financial rewards. One week she mentioned a desire to travel, and the next week she returned to tell me about an offer she had received to visit France for three weeks, all expenses paid, as the guest of a business partner.

She accepted the offer knowing she never would have gone if she hadn't been separated from her husband. Within days, she came across an old journal and marveled at a twenty-year-old entry that read, "I want to travel to France, visit castles, eat, drink, be happy, and make new friends—especially French friends."

And that's almost exactly what she did! Except, she didn't just visit a few castles; thanks to her business connections, she was able to stay overnight in a variety of exclusive castles closed to the general public. She also made many French friends with whom she cooked and shared incredible meals.

The more she followed her heart and her own intuition, the more her life unfolded in amazing ways. Meanwhile, her emotional pendulum had begun to hover calmly near the equilibrium position.

Then came the eleventh month. That gently swaying pendulum caught a strong winter wind and took flight. "I'm panicking," she tells me. "I went to my doctor thinking I was having a heart attack, and she said I was having a panic attack. I'm angry. I'm out of control. I can't tell you the last time I slept for more than three hours."

"Yikes! Hang in there." That's not really what I say, but my actual words are about that insightful. Still, "hang in there" is what I believe. She is getting closer to her truth, to her decision. My hunch about this sudden, wild swinging of her emotional pendulum is that it will be short-lived, as will its symptoms, including the solitary panic attack.

Three weeks later, she arrives for her session with clarity as an evident companion. "I did it. I knew it was right, and I asked for the divorce. It was so strange. I met a friend for lunch. We've both had heavy things happening, so we decided that we'd have a problem-free lunch. Like the old days. We'd ordered our food and were chatting when all of a sudden I said to her, 'I know what I have to do, and I have to do it now. I need to ask him for a divorce. I can see clearly that it will be best for both of us.' My friend just listened and then asked, 'So should I get your lunch to go?'

"He was calm about it. Hurt, of course, but we were on the same page. It was time. My emotional pendulum had been still for a while. It took one last crazy swing higher than ever before, and then I solidly hit the equilibrium position."

"There's a fancy word for that," I say, smiling. "*Clarity*. It allows us to walk through anything and create everything."

"Yes," Suzanne says, "you told me when I got here I'd also find freedom and vitality. I didn't believe you, but it's true. I experienced it for myself. And everybody can see it, even my family members who were so angry and aloof when the separation happened."

She pauses before continuing, "But there is something that I never could have expected, something that can't be seen but can absolutely be counted on. Now I trust that the unknown is faithful." We ended our session, after nearly a year's worth of weekly sessions, with a hug and deep mutual respect.

Later I marvel at her comment, "Now I trust that the unknown is faithful." Every time a client has moved courageously into the unknown, scary, old messaging pops up, trying to convince us things won't work out. But again and again, I have witnessed how moving courageously into the unknown in search of a better life prompts a deep and mystic awareness to arise from within. Moreover, when we dare to take action based on integrity and authenticity, opportunities that we never dreamed possible appear. From a place of needing to know and needing to control, we move into a more natural rhythm where not knowing is perfectly fine. Not only do we not need to know it all, but we can trust that what is unknown is faithful to our healthy desires. In fact, the unknown is faithful to our happiness beyond our wildest imaginings.

${\bigcirc}$ Tool! The Emotional Pendulum Review

- The bigger a decision's impact, the higher the emotional pendulum will swing.
- Notice which emotions occupy the highest points of the pendulum.
- Recognize that the emotional pendulum will settle if given time.
- Waiting for the emotional pendulum to land near the equilibrium position will result in clarity.
- Clarity will allow you to make a positive decision and walk through the hard stuff with grace and ease.

Finding You in Your Relationships

Rebecca is bummed. On the outside she seems fine, but inside, within her most intimate relationship—the one she has with herself—she is miserable. "It used to be that other people—friends, family, coworkers, a random person in the mall—made me nervous," she explains. "I had a talking doll when I was a kid, and when you pulled the string, she would say phrases like 'I have butterflies in my tummy' and 'I'm just afraid of everything!' And that's exactly how I felt! Maybe that's why I loved that doll so much ..."

"Shrinking Violet!" I exclaim. "I loved her too! Although looking back, she was so nervous and sad; she had zero self-confidence."

Rebecca laughs. "Yeah, she was a hot mess! Nothing like the smug, self-satisfied, 'I'm amazing!' dolls that my children have today. I used to think that doll was the only one who really understood me," she says almost wistfully. "But now all those relationship issues are gone. I like spending time with my friends, family, husband, and even the people at my work. It's the internal stuff that's all messed up now."

She starts to list off her problems: "I can't eat right. And I drink too much. I've tried diets and AA, but they only made me more miserable. With the dieting I'd get skinny, but then as soon as I stopped dieting, I'd get way fatter! What a joke. As for AA, after sitting through a meeting, I'd immediately text all my friends to see who wanted to go out for drinks. Another joke—on me! Oh, and get this: I just finished my master's degree in nutrition! With honors! I'm a living comedy hour."

"Gaining weight, drinking too much, and now you have a degree that's bogus." I slowly consider each problem aloud before adding perkily, "Well, at least you haven't lost your sense of humor."

Suddenly Rebecca isn't laughing anymore. In fact, she looks mad. "Excuse me? Are you even listening? I know I have a great insurance plan, but what does my insurance company even pay you for?"

"Sometimes I wonder that too," I muse. "But enough about me; let's get down to your relationships."

"Okay, really? I knew you didn't get it!" Rebecca is growing angrier.

Before she becomes completely exasperated, I get serious: "Humor me a minute. What if we looked at your messiness with food and alcohol as relationships?"

I remind Rebecca that she used to be an emotional see-saw around her friends, family, and coworkers: bouncing between false confidence, extreme insecurity, and angry rebellion. Her relationships were unbalanced and exhausting at best and resulted in dramatic misunderstandings at worst. I remind her that she successfully found ways of creating boundaries and enjoying her relationships.

"Okay, I get what you mean," Rebecca nods. "This does feel similar. I don't have those people problems anymore, but I still feel that way about food. One minute everything's okay, but the next minute it's terrible! I become like an overly critical parent, demeaning myself in the hopes that criticism will help me make smart choices. Then when that backfires, I rebel and eat out of control. With the booze, it's a little different. If I were to compare it to a relationship, it would be like having good sex with a bad guy.

It's all fun in the moment, but afterward you feel scummy. And obviously he doesn't really care about you."

Out of aggravation comes a plea for moderation and a desire for freedom.

"It's funny," I note. "Not the bad sex part—although that can be funny too, but I digress ... It's funny to me that when you put a sunflower seed in the dirt, it automatically becomes a sunflower. And when you bring home a kitten, it naturally grows into a lazy old cat. But human beings, we aren't guaranteed to grow into our full potential; we have to work at it. First we bump around, failing miserably, and then we try things again, continuously learning in an effort to become our best selves. It doesn't just happen. And that's the beauty of choice: we can reflect on past mistakes and choose to act differently in the future."

Rebecca looks half-convinced, so I continue. "The same holds true with food and alcohol. The kind of relationship you establish with each of these will have consequences, which we learn about through trial and error. For instance, if you eat way too much, you might find yourself spending a lot of money on a new wardrobe. If you drink way too much, you might lose your driver's license, and some self-esteem to boot. But there's no reason to beat ourselves up; in fact, that usually keeps us from learning, since we're too busy searching for a big enough stick with which to club ourselves."

I can see Rebecca is connecting with my theory, so I keep going. "Instead of slandering ourselves, we might try examining the results of our choices and letting those guide our future decision making in order to bring about the consequences we desire. For instance, our grandmothers and science both say that a balanced diet—one with a variety of foods eaten in moderation—is the best way to achieve a healthy body, increase our energy, and expand our creativity. As a master nutritionist, you know that scientific research—and our grandmothers—have found that diets don't work. In fact, people almost always regain more weight than they lose. And they lose heart as well when they realize that being thin doesn't lead to happiness and that they denied themselves for no reason."

"Oh, yeah!" remembers Rebecca. "Nothing like being thin and unhappy to send ya to the store for a pint ... okay, two pints of Ben and Jerry's New York Super Fudge Chunk."

"Don't forget the frozen pizza," I add.

"Do I look like someone who's ever forgotten the frozen pizza?" she asks rhetorically. She has put on sixty pounds in the last two years.

I pause and consider—and then reconsider—talking about her weight gain. Instead, I propose, "Why don't we think of food and alcohol as friends? They have the potential to be good ones or bad ones. When you're hanging out and having a good time, it's easy get swept up in the moment and think, *This friend is awesome. I love hanging out with them. We should do this all the time!* But try to remember how you feel *after* hanging out with them. If you still feel good, wonderful! But if you don't, then it's time to think about ways you can spend time together that don't end up making you feel bad. If you can't, then it's time to say goodbye to that friend.

"I want you to work on your boundaries so that you can stay present in the presence of any person or thing without breaking down or compromising yourself—without feeling 'icky' afterwards. It's like how too much food, alcohol, drugs, sex, or TV leaves us with a hangover. But there's no such thing as trusting ourselves too much. It's joyous to wake up feeling good about ourselves, our integrity intact, knowing we have made healthy choices."

"I seriously get it," Rebecca says.

"Good," I reply. "To stay in integrity, it helps to understand the difference between intention and impulse." And then I pull out my trusty whiteboard.

🍴 Tool! How to Distinguish Between Intention and Impulse

Intention	Impulse
Sense of clarity, clear choices, and direction	Sense of urgency
Sense that things will be okay; a gentle confidence about the present and the future	Freaking out because you fear your needs won't be met
Feeling relaxed	"Gotta have it, now!"
Filled with joy, peace, and purpose	Scurrying around; filled with anxiety, nervousness, and a sense of doom
Feeling balanced and whole	Feeling out of balance; going to extremes

Two weeks later an energetic Rebecca shows up for our appointment. "Treating food and alcohol like a relationship has helped me be way more conscious when I eat!" she reports. "I'm trying to spend time with each meal to get to know all the ingredients. I think about how the lettuce, the tomato, and the pasta got to my plate. I actually stop to taste and appreciate each bite that goes into my mouth. And I'm not doing the old deprivation thing either. I even had a slice of pizza today. It was amazing."

"Glad to hear it," I grin. "Plus, now we know what your insurance company pays me for."

Rebecca laughs, "Cheers! I'll not drink to that!"

🍴 Tool! How to Find You in Your Relationships

- Acknowledge that you are free to make choices about all of your relationships.
- Recognize that each choice will come with a set of consequences.
- Reflect on your relationships with people, places, and things; identify when the consequences of those relationships make you unhappy.
- Consider opportunities for creating boundaries and setting healthy limits.
- Know that change takes effort.
- Celebrate each positive change.
- Recommit if you have a setback, but don't beat yourself up.
- Help yourself to make the best choices by learning the difference between intention and impulse.
- Appreciate the moments of joy that accumulate when you find and honor yourself in your relationships.

How to Recover from
Extreme People Pleasing

"I've decided I'm going to the Olympics," Katy announces. "I'll be competing in a brand new sport, and I'm goin' for the gold, baby!"

"What's the new sport?" I ask.

"Extreme people pleasing!" she replies. "Check out the smile I've been practicing for the photos." She gives me a toothpaste-commercial-worthy, ear-to-ear, fake smile.

"Hmm, that's pretty good, but …" I hesitate. "I'm not buying it. Your eyes aren't smiling."

"Drat!" she says, frowning with false frustration. "Back to the drawing board."

"Well, wait a second. Let's not give up on the gold so easily! What kinds of payoffs are you getting from your hard work and training in extreme people pleasing?" I inquire.

Katy drops the fake emotions and sighs. "Honestly? A whole lot of anger, exhaustion, and overwhelming depression. I feel like I'm constantly being taken advantage of, like everyone wants something from me. Sometimes I get so down that I just want to hide out so they can't take what little is left of me."

"Anger, exhaustion, feeling taken advantage of, and depression—that sounds like an Olympic-sized payoff but an extremely negative one," I note. "When did you first start feeling this way?"

Katy's eyes narrow, and then it comes to her. "Charm school!"

"Charm school?" I repeat in disbelief. "Please don't take this the wrong way, but you seem like the intelligent, outdoorsy, engineer type. I can't picture you in charm school."

Katy sighs, "I know, I couldn't picture myself there either. But when I was nine or ten, my mom said I had to start ballet or charm school. I actually picked ballet, but after the first class, the snobby teacher with her perfect bun pulled my mom aside. That night, my mom told me I was going to switch to charm school."

I cringe slightly. I've had many snobby teachers, and their secretive conversations hurt. We might need to delve deeper into this topic later, but I decide to move the discussion in different direction for now.

"Okay, so now I have this image of you walking in heels with a book on your head. Was it like that?" I ask.

"Yep, and learning how to sit just so. It was totally unnatural and ridiculously uncomfortable. Everything was so over the top and awful. But my dad backed up my mom's decision, so I was stuck."

"Was that the way it worked around your house?" I ask. "Did your dad usually back up your mom?" I am working hard to avoid the classic counselor-in-training phrase "Tell me about your parents" which I intensely dislike.

"That's what made it even worse!" she explained. "My dad always had the final say in any decision, but for some reason he caved on this one, which totally confused me, since my dad always told me that using my intelligence was the most important thing I could do in life." I can tell that Katy is digging up memories she hasn't thought about in decades, and she pauses to sort through them.

"One day, I was combing my hair in my mom's mirror and practicing some hairstyle they had taught us in charm school when my dad walked in and started scolding me. He told me I was too interested in my looks, and then ..." Katy trails off, and her eyes fill with tears. "He said I was a disappointment because I turned out so shallow. But I was just trying to be pretty like my mom and the teachers at school." I see sadness and then frustration flash across her face.

"He shouldn't have said that. It wasn't even true!" she blurts out angrily. "I was always a hard worker and a great student, both as a little girl and as a grown woman. I never stopped developing my intelligence."

"I can see that. But right now we're just trying to explore events in your past; we don't need to blame or excuse anyone. Can we keep going with this a bit longer to help me understand your experience?"

"Yeah. And I get the no blaming. I mean, he was only human," she reasons. "And you know, we did fix our relationship before he died. We both changed so much; by the end we were really close."

"That's wonderful. What a great accomplishment for each of you," I say.

She nods, her mouth quivering a little.

"So let me get this straight: every Saturday you'd teeter off to charm school in ridiculous shoes and then come home and spend the rest of the week trying not to think too much about yourself?" I ask with one eyebrow raised.

"Yeah. It was pretty weird," she says.

"Can you see how that might have given you a bit of a divided sense of self?"

"You could say that. Everything in my life was sort of divided, actually," Katy responds.

"Well, we've got a drawing for that!" I retort as I step up to my trusty whiteboard.

🍴 Tool! The Emotionally Balanced Person

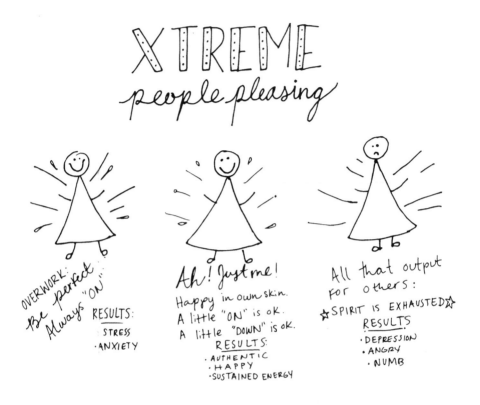

"The first triangle-girl is you as a gold-medal-winning extreme people pleaser. She performs all the charm school skills in an over-the-top, unnatural way. We'll call her the EPP Girl. She gets a too-big smiley face.

"The third triangle-girl is you after burning out from being an extreme people pleaser. She is angry, exhausted, and depressed and feels pretty despondent. We'll call her Dejected Girl. She gets a sad face.

"The second triangle-girl is you when you feel natural and relaxed. She's drawn in a different color but also radiates a bit of the colors from the first and third girls. That's because it's normal to get a little down sometimes, and it's also okay to add in some peppy, over-the-top EPP accents, as long as they feel natural to you.

We'll call her Bright Girl, since the genuine you is both intelligent and glowing.

"If you do too much extreme people pleasing (like the first girl), you'll catapult into the downward spiral of Dejected Girl (the third girl). So the task is to make peace with the second girl, which represents your natural, true self. When you make peace with your true self, your authentic charm can shine through." I finish explaining and smile at her.

Katy is pensive. She asks, "So if I make peace with my true self, I won't feel so angry and exhausted?"

"Exactly," I answer.

"And my true self can have a little bit of people pleasing in there as well? Because, you know, I do love helping people and making them happy when I can," Katy muses, working through these new ideas.

"Yes, you can still do plenty of things to support other people," I confirm.

"Okay, but here's the hard part: what if I do feel angry, but it's justified? Do I have to hide that anger? How do I express it?" she asks.

"It is absolutely okay to feel angry, and you definitely shouldn't hide it. It's healthy to express our anger, but the key is to approach the situation with the goal of finding a solution," I clarify.

"That sounds like a much better way to live. In fact, the only downside I can see is no more gold medal for me!" Katy jokes.

"Not so fast, my fine Olympian friend," I caution. "Perhaps you need to consider a different event. How about becoming a champion in self-knowledge? That way you'll be polishing the real gold—the golden goodness of your unique, true self."

Katy does a great Southern accent as she replies, "Why, that sounds sincerely charming. We certainly must look into that." She starts laughing and then gets thoughtful. "I guess I learned to chase someone else's idea of charming, because in my mind it has nothing to do with balancing a book on my head. I always felt most charming when I was just being myself. I've worked hard, and I always try my best to be a good friend. Those are the things that matter to me, so I don't know why I'm still doing the equivalent of trying to stumble around clumsily in uncomfortable shoes in order to live up to someone else's idea of 'good enough,' especially since I wear fashionable flats and use an e-reader these days anyway! I hope no little girls are learning how to balance an e-reader on their heads!"

She stops and reflects for a moment before continuing. "All this time, I've been a champion of charm—just me as I am—and I didn't even know it!"

"And in knowing it now, you win the gold!" Because I don't have a lot of gold medals hanging in my office, I open my bamboo tea container and ceremoniously present her with my favorite tea. In my best Wizard (from the Wizard of Oz) voice, I proclaim, "I hereby name you the 'Champion of Charm' and award you this Infused Vitality Tea."

⚇ Tool! Become an Olympic Champion of Self-Knowledge

- Mixed messages from our childhood can result in behaviors that foster a divided self-image.
- A divided self-image often results in overworking ourselves to please others.
- Spending too much energy trying to please others can backfire and result in depression and despondency.
- Elements of our divided self can be incorporated into a healthy expression of genuine self.
- One way to know if you're expressing your genuine self is if you feel genuinely at ease.
- We are truly charming when we are being our true selves.
- Remember these wise words from Oscar Wilde: "Be yourself. Everyone else is already taken."

Part Four: Counseling Can Help You Ask Important Questions

The Art of the Pause

Clients have lots of questions, and I do my best to provide them with quality answers. Here are some of my favorite frequently asked questions:

Q: You actually get paid for doing this?

A: Yep. I take cash, check, credit card, or insurance.

Q: If you had to boil it down, what is the most important thing I could learn in therapy?

A: Good vibes. How to feel them about yourself, and how to share them with others. Literally, learning techniques to live your life with a higher, more positive and playful vibration.

Q: Okay, therapy has helped me to "know thyself," feel good about who I am, and act positively toward others. Still, I wonder, what's the most important thing therapy can help me learn to *do*?

A: [I take a deep breath in and out] Pause.

Q: Pause?

A: [I take another deep breath in and out] Pause.

People come to therapy because they are experiencing intense emotions and need help dealing with them. So in order to understand what therapy can do for us, it's helpful to first explore the nature of emotion. Let's take a look!

🍴 Tool! Emotion and the Art of the Pause

E / motion

ENERGY! + expression

FEELING: intense urgent { + SIMULTANEOUS } expression = Uh-Oh!

TOOL: create pause

E (energy) { PAUSE } motion (expression)

= GREAT CHOICES!

The English word *emotion* is derived from the French word *émouvoir*, which comes from the Latin word *emovere*. In Latin, the *e* means energy, and *movere* means motion. Now let's break it down for modern eyes and ears. At this point in the session, I usually grab my handy dark-blue marker and head for the whiteboard to draw the following tool.

First I add a slash in-between *e* and *motion*. *E* is all about energy. Our various emotional states create energy, and the greater the emotional experience, the greater the amount of energy we will feel surging through our bodies. Motion, on the other hand, has to do with movement and action. In this case, motion is how we express the energy that arises from our feelings.

The best thing you can learn to do in therapy is to put a pause between the energy of your emotions and the action that follows. This helps with everything from self-harm and addiction to issues in our relationships, our work or at school.

Yet the art of the pause is an overlooked idea for most of my clients. Overlooked mostly because not too many of us have been taught to think about and use this simple yet very effective tool. Instead, too often we take action just seconds after feeling an intense emotion. Here, we mistakenly believe that our energy must be expressed as soon as possible. Here are some examples:

- You are cut off in traffic and retaliate by tailgating.
- Your ideas are overlooked by your boss in a meeting, and so you immediately start belittling said boss to your coworkers.
- You put on an outfit you love, and when your partner makes a disparaging comment, you either lash out with an equally hurtful remark or give him or her the silent treatment.

Our whiteboard drawing shows a line between the energy of the emotion and its expression. The best choices are made when there is time to pause and consider all possible options before taking action. Many clients understand the value of the pause but don't know how to actually implement it. This is when I grab a red marker and amend what is written on the whiteboard:

E (energy) {PAUSE!} Motion (expression)

Now that the formula is clearly presented, the only things missing are concrete tools for achieving the {PAUSE!}. Here are six of the most successful pause techniques I know:

1. The Lifesaver Tool (Created by W. Doyle Gentry, PhD)

When you are experiencing a strong emotion, suck on a Lifesaver and wait until it dissolves (no chewing!) before taking any action. This will take Type-A folks about four minutes and the rest of the population about six minutes. While that sounds like a short amount of time, what you are likely to do four or six minutes after your initial emotional response is drastically different than what you are likely to do immediately after feeling strong emotions.

To understand why this tool is so helpful, consider that the sucking response is one of the first actions we perform as babies; we quickly learn to associate it with comfort and sustenance. Also, while a Lifesaver doesn't have a lot of calories, it does have a pleasant, sweet taste. Experiencing this range of associations—sweetness and comfort—right when we're also feeling a surge of anger or sadness, for instance, is confusing for our human brains and forces us to pause. When you're wound up, buying a little time for your brain is priceless.

2. The Sniff Tool (Created by J. LaPointe, PhD in life)

Go outside and take a sniff. Actually, take three of them—breaths, that is. Let your body take the lead in helping you relax. Most intensified emotional states produce contractions in the body and constriction of the blood vessels. Deep breathing does the opposite by helping your body relax and your blood vessels expand. Since our minds and bodies are interconnected, you'll find your mindset also relaxes and opens to new possibilities.

3. The I-Need-a-Moment Tool

When you are experiencing a strong emotion, recognize it as a red flag. This is not the time to spew your hurt, anger, or frustration. Nor is it the right time to act impulsively, even though it might feel like the perfect opportunity to let it all out. When you feel this way, say, "I need a moment." We often get so focused on solving issues right away that we forget it is perfectly appropriate, and often necessary, to take a moment. State your need for a little time, and then distance yourself from the situation until you're able to return with a calmer, more level-headed approach.

This tool has four steps:

A. Request a pause.
B. During the pause, engage in self-care. For example, go for a walk, have a cup of tea, or take a bath. Do whatever you need to do in order to relax your body and mind.
C. When you've calmed down, reflect on the other person's experience. Can you see why he or she felt hurt or became angry? Can you appreciate the other person's point of view and emotional response?
D. After all parties have had the chance to go through steps A-C, regroup with the intention of starting a positive dialogue, developing a deeper understanding, and producing creative solutions.

If you need help starting the dialogue or producing positive solutions, make an appointment with a counselor.

4. The Let's-Start-Over Tool

This one works well for couples but has also been used successfully for professional and family relationships. The tool is just what it sounds like: when two (or more) people are having a conversation and things begin to head south, the couple makes an agreement to start over. One person walks out of the room and each person takes a few deep breaths. Then they reenter the situation with the intention of creating a new, different, and more compassionate exchange.

The catch for this tool is that all parties involved must acknowledge that they have fallen into an unpleasant, unhealthy, or unproductive pattern and decide to explore this tool for the sake of improving the relationship. Once there is buy-in from all parties, the "Let's Start Over" tool can be incredibly helpful.

One of my favorite real-life examples of this tool was a couple who would always fight right when the husband came home from work. When they were first using this tool, he'd go outside and then come back in the front door as if for the first time. If they started fighting again, he'd go outside and come back again and again, up to three times. For them, the third time was the charm; after the customary two false starts, they began to experience evening after evening of connection. As time went on, they were able to get it right the first time around. They went from "I can't take it" to "we can make it" using this tool.

5. The Do-Anything-Else Tool

When you're at your wit's end, overcome with emotion, and ready to lash out, you can create a pause by doing anything other than what you're about to do. Stand on your head, sing a song, recite a poem, or take a walk. And keep standing on your head, singing that song, reciting that poem, or taking that walk until you feel confident you can choose to take an action that will have a positive outcome. This isn't rocket science, but it's definitely challenging. Not only will this technique help you stay out of trouble, but it will also allow you the chance to pause and love yourself. Give yourself permission to be less than perfect. Give yourself space. Give yourself grace.

6. The Play-Dead Tool

A client once asked me, "What do I do if none of the other pause tools work for me?"

I answered, "Play dead."

The client looked stunned, but I said, "Don't knock it till you've tried it."

Sometimes people go through extreme experiences. Maybe you feel bored, provoked, tired, sad, lonely, and angry all at once, or maybe there are a host of other emotions that are hitting you on a grand scale. When this happens, I think of a comic strip that shows two couples at a dinner party. The hosts are so hopelessly bored yet stuck that they lie down in the middle of their living room and play dead. The other couple slowly notices and makes the decision to leave. When push comes to shove, when you don't know what to do, when you only know you don't want to exacerbate a bad situation, just play dead. Hit the floor. It may not be the most elegant solution, but it will save you heartache. It might also save your relationship with another or relationships within your career.

Finally, it's important to recognize that using these tools to make space for a pause not only protects and honors the people around you but can also help you to discover that the pause-worthy person is you. Pause. And your true presence appears.

Measuring Up: Three Sessions in Search of One's Soul

At the start of our first session, John rages, "I just can't measure up. It makes me angry, and then I lash out. Next thing you know, I've dug a giant hole for myself, and I can't get out."

By the end of our first session, he seems relieved and says, "I thought you were going to tell me that I was worthless and that there was no hope for me. See you next week."

At the start of our second session, John rages, "I just can't measure up. It makes me angry, and then I lash out. I keep digging a giant hole for myself, and then I fall in and can't get out."

By the end of our second session, he admits, "I can see hope for me." But just as I'm getting excited, he adds, "I'm just not sure how I'll ever overcome feeling so worthless."

At the start of our third session, John rages, "I just can't measure up. It makes me angry, and then I lash out. I just keep digging myself deeper and deeper into a hole. Please help me get out."

I'm dismayed that he's still repeating his "I can't measure up" mantra and has made so little progress, so I pull out my best material. We review cognitive behavioral therapy, which postulates that if you change the way you think, you'll change the way you feel; this will in turn allow you to take positive action. We review our discussions from our first and second sessions, focusing on belief systems, their outcomes, and our abilities to change them. We even review mindfulness techniques, but nothing seems to work.

By the end of our third session, I say, "I can tell you understand these ideas. Yet I can also see that nothing is moving you. Have you been practicing any of the tools we've discussed?"

To his credit, John responds honestly, "I know I should, but no, I haven't. But I'll try this week, really."

His words are well intentioned—I suppose they are meant to make one or both of us feel better—but like eggs entering the frying pan, they land with a splat. Though we are nearing the end of the session, John sinks deeper into the overstuffed, forest-green chair. He looked far more miserable than when he walked in the door, which demonstrates exceptional powers of self-defeatism.

Remembering lesson number one from graduate school—talk about what's there—I tell him, "You look miserable."

Without skipping a beat, John replies, "I am."

Thinking practically, I realize there are only eight minutes left in our session. Intellectually, I'm out of options. Emotionally, I'm stuck. And spiritually, I feel bankrupt. Wait a minute, I think. I'm not spiritually bankrupt! What is that disconnect?

I look at John. He's feeling too terrible to notice that most of the conversation in the room has been happening inside my head. I finally address him, "This might sound odd, but do you pray? Or do you have a connection to something larger than yourself that you trust?"

John sits up, looks momentarily surprised, and then disappears into the overstuffed chair again. "I did," he sighs, "but now that you mention it, I don't think I have said a prayer since I had a very bad interaction with my mother eight years ago. I felt like such a shit; I felt so unworthy. I couldn't pray at all after that."

I weigh my words carefully before gently responding, "Your misery is not a punishment for being a bad person; it is your wake-up call to trust in something larger than yourself. Being part of the world and trusting that you have something to contribute, that's key to our humanity. Of course that doesn't mean it's not a struggle. In fact, many people feel deeply conflicted about whether they should dedicate their energies completely to serving others or pursue their personal passions. However, a balanced, fulfilling life requires both sides; once we realize this, we can unlock unlimited imagination, creativity, and joy. To accomplish this, however, we need to be connected spiritually. Now I'm not advocating for any religion in particular; I'm just suggesting you search for a spiritual connection that resonates with you. So for this week, your homework is to pray."

John stares at me, his eyes wide and his body leaning toward me. In a half whisper he wonders aloud, "How can I? How can I pray when I'm worthless? When I can't measure up?"

I'm moved by his raw emotion and the willingness that is inherent in his body language and whisper. I say, nearly as softly, "Start with the prayer to be able to pray. Pray to empty your cup of misery, and fill your cup with self-love. Pray to get past 'measuring up,' to be done with that concept."

By the end of our third session, John promises, "I'll practice every day, and I'll let you know how it works." His statement sounds like the beginnings of a prayer to me. The magnificent sound of tentative but courageous willingness fills my office. John looks relieved and the tiniest bit happy. Spontaneously, he half-smiles. When he stands up, his footsteps are lighter. As I watch him exit my office, I see a human being worthy of respect and ready to engage in the universal dance of life.

﹛◯﹜ Tool! How to Measure Up When You Think You Don't

- Feeling worthless means not believing in our own generosity, goodness, talents, compassion, and worthiness.
- Feeling worthless is caused by a separation from something larger than ourselves—call it Jesus, Allah, the Universe,

the Divine, Nature, A sense of Awe, or whatever you prefer. As humans, we long for a connection to something greater, and we are made whole to the extent that we seek, find, and trust in this two-way relationship. A healthy relationship with something larger than ourselves fosters respect for our own lives, the lives of other people, and the endless forms of life on our planet.

- Our deepest joys come from being able to experience awe for ourselves and being of service to others. Many of us struggle with how to balance enjoying life with being of service until one sweet day we realize that we need to do both and that by doing so, we can fully and deeply participate in life.

Part Five: Counseling Can Help You Improve Your Relationships

The Hallmark Card You'll Never Send

Dave and Donna are at it again. They arrive for their Saturday morning marriage counseling appointment right on time, furious with each other. This is so standard that a surreal nonchalance fills the air. As usual, they're at total odds. It's emotionally heated, and of course, both of them are red-faced. But most importantly, the more she raises her voice, the more he retreats.

I retreat momentarily into the kitchen and return with three cups of tea, confident that the fight will provide fruitful fodder for our session. That is, I have faith that the fight will get resolved and that in the process, they will gain a deeper understanding of each other along with more effective communication skills.

And that's exactly what happens. In fact, they take a particularly poignant step in this session by discovering what lies beneath their fights: fear. Dave wants Donna to recognize his love for her and his willingness to support her. It's important to him that she see his efforts to be helpful and considerate of her needs.

When she responds, "I do see your efforts. I do believe in your love. And I love you too," there is a palpable flow of positive energy between them.

That flow increases when Donna admits that she picks fights with Dave when she is overwhelmed. She feels herself becoming "a control freak" and hates it. It's important to her that Dave recognizes she is only one person but that she is trying to make everything nice for everybody.

He tells her sincerely, "You pull everything off beautifully, but I want to make it easier on you, I'll do anything to help lighten all the expectations you feel weighing on you."

When he says this, it is like watching a time-lapse video on National Geographic—one moment Donna is a tightly closed bud, and the next, she's a radiant rose in full-bloom.

So why are they here, in counseling, on a lovely Saturday morning? They are here because a marriage that had gone very well for many years had slowly and subtly become one in which things were not going well at all. But they are also here because, despite their diverging experiences, they were both willing and able to come together and say, "I want to do what it takes to stay together and both be happy."

This coming together of willingness reminds me of confluences in nature. I frequently draw upon examples from nature and the physical world in my sessions because, as humans, we exist in these worlds, and they are far more interesting and effective teachers than any amount of psychobabble will ever be.

I ask Dave and Donna to consider the confluence in some nature scenarios. I begin by telling them that there are moments when two streams meet and begin to flow together. The streams spring from different points on a high mountaintop, following on their own imperatives, until suddenly they run into one another in a random and surprising manner. They are happy to join together, feeling the delight of extra energy as they cascade through the lovely landscape.

"Like when we literally bumped into one another in the grocery store," Dave interrupts.

"That was how we met," Donna elaborates.

Other times, when two streams intersect, they churn and mix together uneasily while creating furious, turbulent rapids. I recall lying on my belly watching just such a river from high atop a cliff in Northern California. The sounds of the violent, watery collisions were profoundly unsettling.

"I bet that's what our arguments sound like," Dave muses.

Another outcome of such a confluence can be the dredging up of sediment from one or both streams. In such cases the sediment from one stream swirls around the other, causing discoloration in both streams. In these cases, the surface is most noteworthy for the lack of blending and the resulting ugly appearance of long buried residue.

"That one sounds familiar too. We certainly can stir up a lot of old dirt in one another," Donna notes.

And yet all over the world powerful streams merge together seamlessly to create crystal-clear rivers that flow with increased vigor. I would call these occurrences confluences of joy.

Dave and Donna are silent.

"Okay, guys," I say, "that's why you're here. You haven't given up on this fourth option. I brought up these scenarios because I know you two like spending time in nature. I also know that Dave is very analytical, so let's turn our nature example into a set of Venn diagrams. This is our framework for talking about the stages through which an intimate relationship cycles."

They seem to like my whiteboard drawings. I once drew two stick figures, and then, to indicate an emotional intention of reaching toward one another, I added long fingers to the stick figures. This prompted Donna to exclaim, "Oh no! Now we look like Edward Scissorhands!" Which they did, in an unintentional and frightening kind of way. Since then, the feeling of potential giggles has filled the air whenever I wield my markers around them.

Conscious of this, I walk to the whiteboard and draw the following four Venn diagrams:

⚔️ Tool! The Marriage/Partner Relationship Cycle

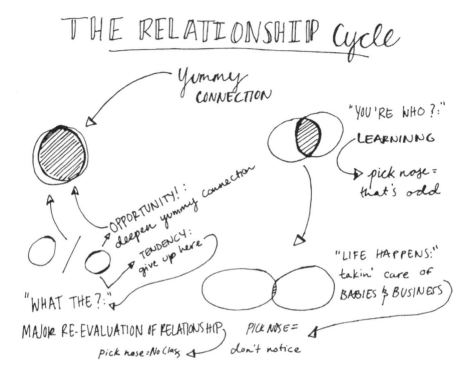

THE RELATIONSHIP *Cycle*

Dave and Donna actually huddle together and lean toward the whiteboard like kids watching cartoons. Dave laughs and smiles at Donna, and she giggles.

First we have the Yummy stage. This is where you fall in love with someone and proclaim to the world, "S/he makes me want to be a better person!" This is where the person picks his or her nose, and you're certain it's the most adorable gesture ever made. In this stage, each person is just starting to get to know a little about the other. There is a lot of yummy connection.

Then there is the "You're who?" stage. This is where you've still got a lot of connection, yet each person is beginning to get a clearer idea of the other's personality and proclivities. This is where you tell your partner, "I didn't know you were such a World War II history buff. How cool that you can talk about each battle in such detail."

But when you see your partner pick his or her nose, you think, *That's odd. I thought s/he had more social savvy.*

Next we move to the Life Happens stage. This is where your connection begins to wane, often because of big life events, like having a child, starting a new job, or going back to school. This is the stage where you might hear your partner's name and think, *Wait, how do I know them? Don't tell me; let me guess.* When your partner picks his or her nose, you're too busy to notice.

Finally, we have the "What the ...?" stage. In this stage, you feel almost no connection to your partner. You're most likely hurt, angry, frustrated, or all of the above. This is where you wonder, *Who is this irresponsible jerk?* You're not thrilled when the answer is "your spouse." You are constantly reevaluating whether you want to stay in the relationship. In this stage, when your partner picks his or her nose, you go batshit crazy.

"The stages themselves are not problematic," I explain, "but our cultural perspective often is." I gesture to the last two drawings and point out, "You will never find a Hallmark card that represents these two stages."

Almost all Hallmark cards are geared toward the Yummy stage. You know, the greeting cards that show us images of "true love." While most people can admit that these cards tend to be pretty silly—unless they themselves are in the Yummy stage, in which case they probably find the cards profoundly moving—at some level we believe that is what love looks like because we're bombarded by similar messages in television shows, movies, and other media. Therefore, once we (inevitably) leave this stage, it can seem like the relationship is doomed. When this kind of cultural messaging is so ever present, it's painful to feel like our reality doesn't live up to the fairy-tale narrative.

Now to be fair, Hallmark is starting to expand its reach by making cards that reflect the "You're who?" stage. The images might not be so picture perfect, but the underlying sentiment of deepening love is still attractive. Hallmark has brilliantly filled these kinds of cards with you-are-my-soul-mate messages. This smooths over the rough patches of differences of opinion and even excuses a little disconnect.

Because there aren't any cards out there that say, "Honey, I just don't have time for you, but I love ya, good ol' what's-your-name," the third stage can feel pretty dicey. And it is. While we can use our smart brains to rationalize that our lack of romance is due to the business, the baby, the boss, and so on—and this may be true to some extent—if you hang out in this stage too long without discussing it with your partner, you'll end up watering the weeds of resentment.

Last, but not least, there is the Hallmark card you'll never send. I'm pointing to the "What the ...?" stage. If such a card did exist, it would simply read, "I want a divorce." By this stage, you don't care if there is a drawing of a cute bear or a dead plant, you just want a card that says, "I want out!"

Here's the memo we didn't get: this is not just the most painful of the four stages; it's also the place with the most opportunity for creating the relationship you want. If you can make it through the tough "What the ...?" stage, you're headed back into the Yummy stage, but with a deeper and more satisfying level of intimacy.

Another memo most of us didn't get before we got married was the one that says all of these phases are normal. So go ahead. Write your own memo and educate yourself. Instead of losing hope, rededicate yourself, along with your partner, to making space for connection, and flow toward a confluence of intimacy and joy.

🍴 Tool! Ways Relationships Reflect the Physical Nature of a Confluence:

- Some streams come together and thereby increase their energy and power.
- Some streams come together and thereby create fury and turbulence.
- Some streams come together and thereby cause sediment to rise to the surface.

- Streams resist coming together when sediment separates them.

❮❍❯ Tool! Lessons from the Hallmark Card You'll Never Send:

- Relationships naturally go through phases.
- We are culturally programmed to panic when the picture-perfect stage of our relationship wanes.
- Keep ongoing and open dialogue a priority, especially when your schedule gets hectic.
- The hardest moments can give rise to the richest opportunities for intimacy and reconnection.

The I'm-Right Routine

Cathy and Ron do not sit next to one another on the long sofa like usual. Instead, he flops onto the sofa, and she flings herself into the oversized chair adjacent to him. He lets out a heavy sigh while his arms dangle limp at his sides. She huffs and crosses her arms over her chest. They take a couple more sighs and huffs, pause, and then simultaneously report, "We're not doing well." Because they are not getting along, speaking in sync is not "cute" to either of them. On the contrary, it provokes a sharp rise in the feeling of agitation that permeates the room. But to me, it's quite noteworthy; for better or worse, there is still enough of a connection between them that they unintentionally speak the same words at the same time.

"So what's going on?" I ask.

"She always has to be right," Ron declares.

At exactly the same moment, Cathy glares and says, "He always has to be right."

I keep my mouth closed and let the fury die out a bit. "Okay, I get the general idea," I say cautiously. "How about a specific example that we can use to work through this issue?"

"You don't have to look too hard to find an example. We can start with this morning. She got so impatient that she jumped out of the car!" Ron accuses.

"Not before you made us so late that I was going to miss my hair appointment," Cathy counters. "All because you insisted you knew where it was—even though you'd never been there. I think I know how to drive to my own hair salon, especially since I've been going there for the last ten years!"

"Well, only one of us is a professional driver, so I thought I knew a better way to get there. If you'd stayed in the car, you would have found out I was right," Ron retorts.

"Only one of us is a professional driver, and only one of us is a professional asshole!" Cathy snips.

"Whoa. That's a stop!" I say. "Number one, name-calling is out of bounds, period. Number two, I've got the gist of it. Now I want each of you to think for a moment. When exactly did the argument begin? We're not looking for a litany of each other's bad behaviors; we're just looking for the moment when things began to go sideways."

"At the corner of Fourth and J Street," they say simultaneously. Then they simultaneously give each other the stink eye.

Cathy continues, "That's when I said, 'Take a left,' and he decided to go straight. So I got out and walked."

Ron adds, "She wasn't very happy when I pulled up in the car at the same time she was walking up the steps."

Cathy corrects him. "I was coming down the steps because I realized that after arguing so much about how to get there, by the time I did get there, I had missed my appointment."

"Then you got back in the car to come here?" I ask.

"I wasn't very happy about that either. No offense," Cathy answers.

"None taken," I respond sincerely.

It's not unusual for one or both people in a couple to be less than thrilled about attending a couples-counseling session. I remember one tall, lanky gentleman whose I'd-like-to-be-anywhere-but-here body language was so loud that I wondered if the three of us would be able to hear anything else. Thankfully that was not the case, and upon leaving, he told me, "That was really helpful."

I smiled and said, "I try to keep the pain to a minimum. Now you can tell your buddies counseling isn't that bad and can even be good."

"Ha!" he laughed. "Thanks for your help, Doc, but none of my buddies are ever gonna know I came here."

One step at a time, I thought. Social stigma doesn't materialize overnight, and likewise it takes time and diligence to overcome it.

I look back at Cathy and Ron. "So you've got a classic case of the I'm-right routine. In the struggle to be right, something important gets tossed aside ... your relationship! In those moments, you become individuals who are only looking out for themselves. The good news is that the cure is simple: remembering. Your task is to remember that marriage is a team sport. We are rooting for the relationship to win."

Noting that they are both quietly listening, I continue, "In this case, you were arguing about whose directions were best, but in reality you were both correct—either path led to your destination. The real wrong turn was when you each made the decision to trust yourselves individually instead of having confidence in your ability to be a great team."

"Team?" Ron grins jokingly.

"What team?" adds Cathy sarcastically. But then she smiles at her husband.

"Exactly," I say. "When things are tough, you need to put your heads and your hearts together and bring your best A game. That's when you want to use your knowledge as a resource to share with your partner—not as resistance to use against each other. Then you can decide together the best play to execute."

When couples are stressed or in trouble, one of the first places to visit is your team roster. If there is only one name on it—yours—then you're only half a team, not really a team at all. If this is happening in your relationship, get out your pencil and add the name of your spouse (or significant other) to the roster. Now you have a whole team. And because true intimacy cuts our sorrow in half and doubles our joy, the real winner is the relationship!

⚏ Tool! Marriage is a Team Sport

- Look at your current issue or problem from a team perspective; make sure your team roster is updated so that both of you are on it!
- Remember: your spouse is on your team. S/he's not the enemy.
- Utilize the resources of the team in problem solving.
- Recognize that an I'm-right attitude will demean the abilities of the team.
- Make a conscious decision to play and win as a team.
- Decide on your next play, and execute it wonderfully, together.

The Idea Guy

Laura and Jim sit comfortably on the couch close to one another. I can see the strong positive energy bouncing between them.

"We had a breakthrough," Laura reports. "You know how Jim is always making suggestions about how to do things better around the house and how, well, I usually don't take them as suggestions but rather as personal criticism?"

I nod.

"Well, this week he said, 'Ya know, Hon, if you put the smaller bowls in the front of the top shelf of the dishwasher and then move the cutlery holder to the far left, you'd increase the dishwasher's loading capacity by nearly 22 percent.'"

I wait, expecting to hear how all hell broke loose after that.

"And you know what I said?" Laura continues. "I said, 'Hey, that's a great idea.'"

"When she said that," Jim chimes in, "we just stared at each other for a moment. Then we both started laughing and couldn't stop."

"That's excellent!" I exclaim. "Congrats you two!"

Three months earlier, a similar event had been the catalyst for beginning couples therapy. Laura was doing the laundry. Jim watched for a moment and then proposed that she could be more efficient by making a couple of simple changes to her laundry methodology. In response, Laura's face turned a deep purplish red as she screamed at him that if he thought she was such an idiot, he could do his own (insert profanity) laundry and, for that matter, his own (insert new, more inflammatory profanity) cooking and, now that she mentions it, his own (insert big-finish profanity) house cleaning. Jim had stared at her, wide-eyed, frozen, and completely confused. Laura knew that her reaction was an overreaction, but her normally cheerful demeanor had been replaced with a previously unknown vileness she couldn't control.

In couples' therapy, it can sometimes feel like there are a lot of people in the room. That's because exploring a couple's issues often requires finding out information not only about the couple but also about their family history, origins, and patterns. We found out that Jim's dad was a matter-of-fact kind of guy—an intelligent aviation engineer who was constantly coming up with a better way of doing everything. Jim's dad never hesitated to share his good ideas, regardless of the situation and with zero attention to the social or emotional context. Jim thought that his dad was cool, so it was cool to act like Dad. And he did. Jim, an intelligent software developer, used his like-dad-ness to find a better way to do almost anything, from car repairs to computer installation to laundry.

When we looked into Laura's dirty laundry, we found that while she was a very high performer academically with a great social network of people who truly adored her, she never felt like she could live up to her dad's expectations. She would strive with all her might, only to receive a flippantly dismissive comment like, "You always get A's. I'm surprised to see this B on your report card." No matter how hard she tried, she could never be smart enough, ergo the delicate scab covering years of rage and disappointment over her lack of praise and support as a child. No wonder she felt wounded when the man in her life made what felt like allusions to her stupidity.

Neither of them were thinking of these subtexts when Laura went deep red with fury over a simple laundry suggestion. So I decided to introduce the Ask-a-Simple-Question tool. Realizing that Jim would probably always be an idea guy, I suggested that Laura ask the simple question that was on her mind: "Are you saying I'm stupid?" We agreed that the asking was not about making Jim lose his mind but was rather grounded in the desire for marital bliss. After a few months of asking this question and hearing sincerely from Jim that the answer was no, Laura no longer heard that she was stupid. Instead, she heard that he had an idea about something that she could either choose to ignore or embrace.

For his part, Jim embraced the opportunity to speak honestly. He looked at her one day and said with deep sincerity, "I think you're brilliant and wonderful. I would never ever call you stupid because I don't want to hurt you. But beyond that, I could never imagine even thinking of you as stupid." The talkative Laura was silent while salty tears flowed down her cheeks. Jim understood her and her feelings; he wasn't her dad.

Yet Jim was a lot like his dad. Once Laura understood the pride and importance Jim placed on offering (unsolicited) solutions to everyone about everything, she relaxed. She also realized that his intentions were loving and kind, which allowed her to trust more deeply in his character and fall back in love with him. More understanding, more trust, more love—now that's a great idea.

¡◯¡ Tool! Miscommunication is Not Malevolence

- Learn to recognize when your reactions are out of sync with the situation.
- Consider that what you heard might not be what was intended to be communicated.
- Ask about what you thought you heard—start with sincere, tone-free, genuine questions like, "It sounded like you said I was stupid. Did you just say I'm stupid?"

- Really listen to the answers to your sincere questions. For example, "No, I just said there's a more efficient way to load the dishwasher."
- Acknowledge the difference between what you heard and what was said.
- Try communicating again, this time experimenting with new ways to express your ideas.
- Take note of, and stop using, any hurtful words that trigger a negative experience for the other person.
- Take into consideration any family of origin dynamics that you (or your loved one) experienced growing up that might be influencing the miscommunication.
- Remember that spouses are not psychics. They can't read your mind, so you'll have to tell them what you're thinking and feeling.

person is just starting to take the first steps of a journey he or she didn't want to take."

I glance at Bill, who is looking at the floor. Trying to sound more encouraging, I say, "It will take time to catch up, but knowing you are working with two different timelines can help you stay sane and focused on working it out."

"So what do we need to do?" Susan asks.

I go on to list various options so that they can choose what works for them. There are the usual things like openness and transparency. After an affair, it is fair for your spouse to request to review your cell phone bills, read your text messages, or visit your social networking sites. It's also important that such activities are engaged in as opportunities to rebuild trust via transparency.

"Every time you find there is nothing to worry about, it's a chance to grow closer," I explain. "Eventually, even the most suspicious spouse gets plain ol' tuckered out from checking so many records. Of course no one gets engaged in a healthy marriage wanting to become a parent to their spouse, but these exercises in transparency are undertaken for the greater good of moving forward. And at the end of the day, that persons spouse has had a chance to prove that he or she is deserving of trust once again."

Because this point is so important, I reiterate, "Transparency activities are set up with the intention of healing the relationship. These are never undertaken with the goal of revenge or shaming the other person. The shame that the cheating spouse feels is already heavy enough to sink the ship, so our emphasis is on helping to keep the boat afloat."

"My boat is a little tippy," Bill warns. "I see that Susan is trying, and I know there are things that I can work on. Yet I just keep getting this bad feeling in my stomach. My head goes nuts, I think of those guys at her work, and ... it's tough."

It is tough.

An extra-special-tough aspect is that the high-spirited, vibrant, and red-haired Susan works for an auto mechanic—that is, she *is* an auto mechanic, not a receptionist or salesperson for the body shop e of the boys. She's gorgeous, and she can talk shop. She not owns her own tools, but she actually knows how to use them. hat's pretty sexy.

an and Bill are looking at me. I've apparently been silent so long while the aforementioned thoughts rumbled around med with the roar of a Big-Block Chevrolet V-8. Then an idea ers forward.

his is a tough situation, but you guys have the willingness, dedication, openness, commitment, and love to make it work. Plus, you genuinely like one another. What might help the most right now is the Experience-Bucket tool. In particular, the 'Is It Okay Now?' process."

go on to describe the human tendency to only believe our own experiences. When we've been through a betrayal—which is a type of trauma—we're naturally afraid that bad things will happen to us again. Most people who have been through a trauma or affair-like betrayal will have triggering thoughts. In this case, the thoughts sound like, *My beautiful wife works with all guys, and I know how they think.* Those thoughts are then going to lead to a bad feeling in your gut, and it's no use trying to talk yourself out of them. So feel them, but also check them against current reality.

As you notice the feelings of insecurity, panic, fear, and anger bubble up, ask yourself, "Am I okay now? Is our relationship okay now?" Usually the answer is yes. Every time you answer yes to that question, you're putting a drop in the "It's Okay Now" Experience Bucket, and drop by drop, as you fill that bucket, your tippy ship will find smooth sailing. You'll slowly learn to trust your new, good experiences.

It's a little cumbersome, to say the least, to mentally reset the sails that many times a day. Yet the effort pays off when you start to feel your relationship sail toward harmony and happiness.

Susan is inspired. She immediately comes up with three ideas of how she can reassure Bill, how she can help him know that it's okay now. Bill looks a little doubtful, yet he lets himself be convinced by the two women in the room beaming it-will-be-great vibes.

In a few months, Bill's "Is It Okay Now?" Experience Bucket is filling up. It's still tough, but he's using the tool to ask himself, "Am I okay now? Is everything in our relationship okay now?" And the answer is always yes.

"Oh hell, no!" Susan recounts. "That's what I said when he decided to get a motorcycle."

"I've learned I'm too nice, too much of a pushover. This is something I've always wanted for myself," Bill replies calmly.

I realize I've forgotten to describe Bill; he is gorgeous and well built and has the most endearing, deep-brown eyes you might ever fall into, I mean uh-hem, see.

"It's true," Susan says, "he puts everyone else first, and he needs to put himself first sometimes. But 900cc is the limit."

"I'm fine with 900cc," Bill agrees.

"It just worries me," Susan continues. "He's a smart rider and a really good one. Still ... I want our kids to have their dad. And I kinda want to hang out with their dad too—for a long, long time." Now Susan's ship is tippy.

Bill reaches for her hand and gently holds it. Then he grins. He's loving, calm, and relaxed when he speaks. "With the bike, I can help you fill *your* 'Is It Okay Now?' Bucket!"

We all laugh. He's not getting back at her; he's moving forward with a deeper sense of himself. He's a responsible and experienced rider. He's even a more responsible and experienced father and husband. But she's not backing down either; she's standing up for herself. Her integrity is still intact after one small fall, and she's setting reasonable limits and loving her man.

As they leave our session, I'm more in love with them than ever. I reflect on the gossipy, tabloid-enhanced consciousness that only thinks about exploiting the horror surrounding affairs. For the tabloids and those who adopt that mindset, an affair can only be followed by disdain and distrust.

Yet Bill and Susan have set sail for deeper, more wonderful waters after the affair. Spending time with Bill and Susan is tabloid free, because their story would never make the divisive she against he headlines.

I'm in no way condoning affairs. They are devastating.

Yet, spending time with Bill and Susan as they heal from an affair makes me wish everyone could be as in love, in sync, and in willingness to recommit to the real-deal parts of marriage as they are, because that's one awesome, uncharted adventure!

🍴 Tool! The "Is It Okay Now?" Experience Bucket:

- First ask yourself: What can I do now? What am I willing to do now?
- Recommit. Be transparent. Forgive.
- Trust your experience. Create opportunities for each person to experience the feeling that "our relationship is okay now.
- Let this new trust build naturally. Don't push the timing.
- Recognize that the problem is a way of making things better, a way to consciously create the relationship of your dreams and reorient your relationship toward harmony and happiness.

Low Down Dirty Love: A Story about Belief and Appreciation

Liz, a news reporter, has been having problems with her husband, Frank. She's got some news to report on that front.

"He's not the same guy I married. I mean, I expected that we would both change, just not like this! Oh brother, am I a dummy. Of course no one can predict how another person is going to change. Might as well try to herd cats. Maybe the problem is me. Maybe I shouldn't have ever married. I mean, Frank is a great guy, and a good guy too. You know what I mean? There's nothing really wrong with him. I hate to say this, but sometimes I wish there was something wrong with him. If only he was a drug addict or ..."

She pauses and looks embarrassed. "Once I even wished he'd have an affair—which he never would because he's too loyal and honest. But if he did have an addiction or an affair, then I could leave him, and no one would question it in a million years. But no! He's decent. I just don't understand why I feel so disappointed in the relationship! I'm probably just a freak. But seriously, what should I do about Frank? I'm totally lost."

She wasn't the only one who was lost. Frank was too; he was totally absent from Liz's point of view. Liz had lost her faith in Frank.

Liz had lost faith in all her previous beliefs about their relationship. When I suggest this, she looks at me with a despairing face.

"You've lost me."

"Well, now that we're all wandering," I say. "Let's see if we can locate some solid ground. What is your most disturbing belief about your relationship with Frank?"

"Easy," she responds. "The idea that I have to do everything. We both have full-time careers that are intense and demanding. But after work I cook, clean, shop, do the laundry, and do the dishes. Instead of enjoying life with a partner, I've just got double the work to do. I really have to get the word out to single girls."

"What word is that?" I ask.

"Think twice," she says with a deadpan face.

"Technically, that's two words," I joke. I'm trying to make her laugh since we both know she's the extremely wordy, talkative sort who can get stuck in her seriousness. But she's also fun loving, and that's the part of her I'm appealing to now. "Just a little smile," I urge, even though we all get that this is serious business. She smooshes her lips together, but a little giggle escapes.

"Okay, let's follow your advice and think twice right now," I propose. "Your current belief is 'I have to do everything.' Since your concern was about you and Frank, let's stick to that. Can you think of an old belief you used to have about him?" I suddenly recall her joy at her engagement and prompt, "What was your belief when you got engaged?"

"Wow, I get all the easy questions today," she smiles. "I believed Frank was the most kind and generous man I'd ever met."

"Now we're getting somewhere!" I enthuse. "We might still be slightly lost, yet I think we've found a way out of the deepest part of the forest."

Out comes my handy-dandy whiteboard. And a tool!

⚔ Tool! The Three Stages of Beliefs.

I write down the following:

Beliefs

1. Be drawn to situations and people that match your beliefs.

2. Find evidence to support your beliefs.

3. Create it or make it happen. Voila! Your beliefs are proven to be true.

"Right now, you believe that you do everything. Frank has somehow become lazy and unmotivated. That's the first part of the tool. You are the one who is doing everything: the work, the shopping, the cooking, the cleaning, the laundry. Can I stop listing all the things you do, because this is making me tired? That's the evidence mentioned in the second part of the tool. Therefore, you are in an environment that reflects back to you the belief that you are the one who does everything. That's the third part of the tool."

"I get what you're saying," says Liz, "But pardon me, that's hardly news."

"Ha!" I say. "Let's get to the 'twice' part of 'think twice'! What if your current belief was aligned more with your original belief about Frank? What if your belief about him *now* was that he is the most kind and generous man you'd ever met?"

Liz looks at me like I might be nuts. "And just how does *that* work?"

"Like everything else we do in here," I respond cheerily. "I want you to do an experiment. For the next week, I want you to spend fifteen minutes twice a day exploring your old belief about Frank— that he is a kind and generous man. And a kind and generous man wouldn't sit by and watch you work yourself to the bone. Here's the hard part: let the new belief that he is the most kind and generous man you've ever met roll around your heart, and find a little room for it in that busy head of yours too. Try to quiet down the part of your brain that is already rebelling against what I'm saying."

I see more of that despairing look. My mind gets lost in semantics for a moment as I interpret her expression. *Des-pair-ing*: an interruption of sorts in the pairing. Now she's looking at me like she's sure I'm nuts.

She says, without the least effort to conceal her sarcasm, "So for half an hour every day, I'm supposed to just think about believing differently? Shall I also see if I can conjure up a fairy godmother and make sure to click my heels together three times?"

"Yes!" I want to say, because who hasn't wondered if a fairy tale could come true. But I see her point. "Okay, let's make it five minutes in the morning and five minutes at night. And yes … well, no …" Now I'm starting to question myself. I take a mental pause. What I want her to do is change the energy of her thinking and her feeling from despair and resentment to hope. In my experience, three things might happen once her energy changes: Frank might spontaneously become more of the man she married; he might flake; or she might decide, with clarity, that she needs to fly solo.

Maybe I should just tell her that and talk about the idea of changing her internal energy. After all, there are plenty of wonderful therapists out there using techniques in which they ask their clients to put an imaginary bunny in their hearts or tap on their bodies while repeating phrases of self-acceptance.

So why aren't I being more direct right now? *Know thyself*, I think and add the sister thought, *Have a clue about your client*. It's the wrong time to talk about moving energy when she's already frustrated and wondering if I get kickbacks from Grimm's Fairy Tales.

"I don't want this to be a fairy tale," I confide. "I'm hoping you'll have a real-life happy ending. Your homework is to picture your belief being true, which isn't such a leap of faith since we're talking about a belief you've held before."

Since she has no sarcastic retort, I continue, "You see, we think our beliefs are truth. Yet the truth is, we are free to choose what to believe. However, it is much harder to become aware of your beliefs and then intentionally choose more beneficial beliefs than to hold onto old beliefs even when they no longer serve you." I speak with confidence because I've seen the process many times, yet I realize that my suggestion to simply choose a belief you'd like to be true is daunting and requires tremendous effort. I try to clarify, "Choosing your best belief is a much greater challenge than going with your assumptions."

"But what if my belief that I do everything is my experience?" she inquires.

"Great question! Now challenge it," I respond.

"How?" she asks.

"This is the easy part! Challenge it gently yet firmly. Remember you have also had the experience of Frank being kind and generous. Is it too much of a stretch to be willing to believe that again?"

Liz sighs, "It all sounds wonderful in here, but I'm doubtful. I guess I can give it a try." There is no trace of hopefulness in her voice.

"Yes! Give it a try!" I try to strike a balance between firm encouragement and perky cheerleader. The look on her face says that I've failed at both.

Thus ends another eighty-minute session. No insightful aha moments. No wondrous singing of archangels as background music. No joyous "See you next week!" said with a sense of connection and enthusiasm. Just a bummed out client leaving my office.

Thankfully, that's not the end of the story. The next week, Liz returns stunned.

"I can't believe what happened. He's doing the laundry. Well, that's not the point, but it's really great. He asked if he could do the laundry. Well, no he didn't. Let's see ... how did it happen? Oh yeah. After four days of my ten minutes of testing a new belief, which was really my original belief that Frank is kind and generous, Frank said—out of the blue—'Do you want some help around here?' I couldn't even believe it, so I asked him what he meant. He said I was doing everything, and it was making him feel really terrible. He said he felt like somewhere along the line I'd decided he couldn't do things well enough, so he watched helplessly as I took over doing everything. Can you even believe it? He felt helpless! I thought he'd gotten lazy and uncaring!"

I nod but say nothing.

She continues, "That made me feel bad, but it also made me want to answer his question about what could he do. So I said, 'The laundry!'

"He responded, 'The laundry?' I confirmed, 'Yes I hate doing the laundry. I hate everything about doing the laundry!' He said, 'I didn't know that.' I couldn't even believe my ears, so I asked him, 'After all this time, how could you not know that I hate doing the laundry?' And he said, 'Because you always do it.'

"Can you believe that?" she asks me. "Because I always do it he thought I loved doing laundry." She's shaking her head. "That's why I love Frank. What you see is what you get. I remembered that he's so good for me when I take myself too seriously. I did the laundry, and everything else, because it needed to be done. I never thought of asking him to help me. I guess I actually went right past the place of asking for help to my assumptions of ... of what. I don't even know. I just know I'm tired of my assumptions because since that day I haven't done a bit of laundry. And I don't miss it!"

She's almost gushing now, "We're both happier. Oh, and get this, I realized he does all kinds of stuff around our home. He takes care of all the computer stuff, which I hate to do. I just want my computer to work, and he makes sure it always does. And he knows I like the kitchen to be clean, so even if the living room looks like a college dorm or man-cave, the kitchen is pristine when I come home. He knows I love that, and he actually does more of the shopping and cooking than I was giving him credit for." She is forced to stop for a breath.

"It's good to breathe, like you're always telling me," she admits. Then she adds, "I realized with all my focus on believing that I do everything, I couldn't see how much he does! It's so weird that now that I believe he is kind and generous, everywhere I look I see evidence of all the wonderful things he does for us. And wait, I'm not saying he's rocketed into perfect status! He's not perfect—he's got plenty of things that still bug me—but I don't need him to be. I'm just so happy to see that what I believed from the start is true: he is kind and generous."

Liz breathes again, this time with a deep inhale and deep exhale. "Here's another thing, and it makes me kinda sad. After the laundry conversation, I was thinking while I practiced my ten minute 'new belief' homework. I was thinking about how much he must be hurting from our disconnect. Ya know, somewhere along the way, I started feeling resentful. I didn't treat him so well, and that's when he stopped treating me nicely too."

She stops talking due to the unexpected interruption of tears.

"I forgot how much I appreciate him. He's so solid. I know he doesn't have the emotional intelligence to talk about these things like I do, but I quit talking. I quit the conversation that I needed to open. Instead of being there for him, I got resentful. Now I can't stop thinking about how wonderful he is. And I really love that he does the laundry!"

I say nothing; instead I reach for the whiteboard.

I write the word *Beliefs*, and underneath it, I write three things:

1. Be drawn to situations and people that match your beliefs.
2. Find evidence to support your beliefs.
3. Create it or make it happen. Voila! Your beliefs are proven true.

We both look at it before I begin talking. "Right now, you believe that you made a commitment to be with a man who is kind and generous. Frank has somehow become loving, caring, and motivated to help you. That's number one. You have help with the domestic tasks you like least and assistance with others so that you've got backup at home! That's number two. You're living in an environment that reflects back to you a loving relationship that's filled with generosity and compassion. That's number three."

"I get what you're saying, and pardon me, but that's hardly news," Liz jokes.

I laugh along with her lightness. Then I pause and inhale and then exhale deeply. "Liz, Frank is a good guy, but humor me a minute and let me congratulate you, because you are the one who made a deep internal change. Your willingness to challenge and replace your beliefs had a great payoff, but the real beauty is knowing that you are strong, powerful, and able to choose your own beliefs. Through all your pain and uncertainty, you stuck it out and tried something new."

"You're going to have to come up with something more newsworthy to tell me," Liz jokes again but not without welling up a bit. She makes an attempt to beat her tears to the punch. "Next thing I know, you'll be talking about moving the material world using my internal energy states."

"Me?" I feign innocence, "I don't think so."

We both rise, and she hugs me.

"See you next week," she says joyfully. There is plenty of connection and enthusiasm in her voice as she exits my office. My ears becoming hyperaware, and I hear the faint but distinct and wondrous sound of archangels singing—creating a glorious soundtrack to life.

ⵣ◯ⵣ Tool! Challenge Beliefs! Part One: You

- What are your most heartfelt beliefs about yourself? If any of these are negative, are you willing to challenge them?
- Refute negativity and embrace positivity by rewriting negative beliefs into positive ones. For example, if you believe "I never get a break in life," you can rewrite that into something more positive, like "I am open to getting a break in life." Or better yet, challenge yourself to remember a time when you have gotten a break in life, and then your rewrite can be "There have been times when I have gotten a great break in life."

- If you're having a hard time, think about what you want to accomplish and let that lead the way to rewriting old beliefs. For example, if you believe "I'm not good at accomplishing my goals," you can rewrite that belief into "When I focus and take action, I can accomplish my goals."

⸭◯⸭ Tool! Challenge Beliefs! Part Two: Relationships

- What are your most heartfelt beliefs about your relationship? If any of these are negative, are you willing to challenge them?
- Refute negativity and embrace positivity by rewriting the negative into a positive. Start by asking yourself the following questions:
  - What do I want to experience in an intimate relationship?
  - When do I feel happy and excited about contributing to the relationship?
  - When do I feel happy and excited about being in the relationship?
- Write down what you want to believe as true from now on—that is, choose your new beliefs.
- Make a day-by-day plan to live out the beliefs you chose.
- Start practicing these new beliefs, and record your progress.
- Don't be worried if and when negativity rises up in your life in an effort to defeat your new beliefs. Instead, write down all of those negative thoughts and feelings; recognizing them is the first step to changing them.
- Seek and express appreciation any time, and any where and every time you feel it.

Part Six: Counseling Can Provide Engaging Metaphors

Ride the Best Bus

Anna can't seem to get off the bus. She's on a circular trip that begins with an argument with her husband and ends with her being alone. She's about to make her fourth loop when I interrupt her.

"Do you want to end up alone?"

We both know she doesn't, which is probably why she sounds a little annoyed when she answers, "Well, I want to stop arguing."

"Not likely to happen," I respond.

Now she's more than a little annoyed. "Why would you say that?"

"Because as long as you're in a marriage, there will be times when you disagree, and it's highly unlikely that those disagreements won't turn into an argument every now and then. But what you can do is change your thinking about it."

"I'm supposed to think arguing is okay?" Now she is downright infuriated. "How do you propose I change the way I think?"

"By riding a better bus!" I proclaim. "Check this out."

🍴 Tool! Ride the Best Bus

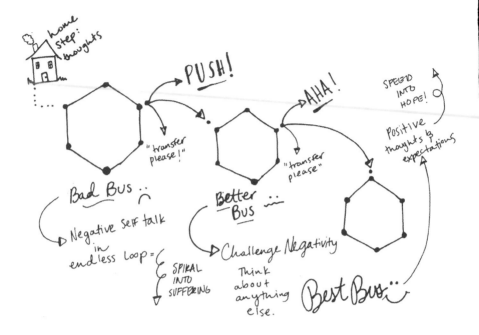

As anyone who has ever taken public transportation knows, when you get on a bus, you do so knowing that you will only be able to get off the bus at the preassigned stops for that specific bus route. Every time you get on that particular bus route, you can know with certainty that you'll always go to the same place. In real life, riding the bus can be an efficient way to get where you want to go. But on the road to self-awareness, the mental bus you're on might not be the right one to get where you want to go.

Right now, Anna is on the wrong bus. She boards this bus by obsessing about her argument, and the next stop is thinking about how she and her husband just can't get along. This is followed by childhood flashbacks of her parents arguing and then moving down the road to remembering the fear of listening to them yell at each other. This catapults her into the express lane as she speeds toward desperation—"I can't be with someone who argues with me this much." Then, as she passes single commuters stalled in traffic, her thoughts stall too. She thinks about how she ends up arguing with everyone she gets close to. Finally she arrives at her destination, which is believing that she will inevitably end up alone, even though that's not where she wanted to go.

She's going round and round on the Bad Bus! You can board the Bad Bus by thinking any of these thoughts, and the route will always be the same, as will the final destination. But here's the good news: almost every bus stop serves multiple routes. Once you become aware of your thoughts and realize that you're on the Bad Bus, you can pull the stop cord and politely ask for a transfer. In this case, though, you don't want a paper transfer; you want a *mental transfer.* After making the decision to disembark the Bad Bus, you can stand up proudly, exit through the folding doors, and wave good-bye as the Bad Bus pulls away.

Then simply get on a Better Bus. At this point, you might not be sure which new bus to ride, but it doesn't really matter; the most important thing is staying off the Bad Bus. Getting a mental transfer can be as simple as reflecting, *I'm thinking about what I don't want. What is it that I do want?* For Anna, that might mean thinking, *I want to get along better with my husband.* And just like that, she's boarding the Better Bus, which takes a totally different route. As she continues riding the Better Bus, she cruises past stops like "What are we arguing about anyway?" and "We're arguing about the stupidest things."

No matter what problem you're dealing with, when you travel past this last stop of seeing clearly the superficiality of your arguments, something amazing happens. It's like waiving your mental transfer in the air and yelling, "Stop, please!" In that moment, the Better Bus screeches to a halt. You bound down the center aisle, jump onto the sidewalk, and promptly bounce up the steps to the third bus: the Best Bus.

Your first stop on the Best Bus is "If we're arguing about stupid stuff, then it's not the stuff we're really upset about." The Best Bus hits the road as you think, *What are we really arguing about?* The Best Bus picks up speed as you think, *Have I hurt his/her feelings?* You fly past stop after stop as you wonder, *Is s/he afraid of something too? Does s/he know that I argue when I'm feeling scared?* Suddenly, just as the Best Bus arrives at its final destination, you do too. It dawns on you, *I think we might be able to use our arguments to get closer to one another.*

In Anna's case, with just two mental transfers, she has gone from thinking that sadness and being alone were inevitable to exploring ways that arguing could actually help her feel closer to her husband. She still has to face the reality of arguing, but look at where it has taken her! Notice that nothing external has changed at all, but her thinking about the situation is significantly different. What happens next is significantly different too.

When she rides the Best Bus, she spirals upward in terms of hope, creativity, and positive action. She feels ready to take steps to get what she really wants. This is exactly the opposite of the Bad Bus, which leads to a downward spiral of hopelessness and helplessness. On the Bad Bus, her actions lacked creativity and were rooted in negativity, which made her willing to accept situations she didn't want.

But it's not just Anna who gets stuck on the Bad Bus. We all do. The more we ride that route, the deeper we ingrain its scenery and sensations into our neural pathways. Of course there's no need to criticize the Bad Bus for following its prescribed route, but there's no need to stay on it either. By challenging ourselves to transfer to a Better Bus, our brains will naturally search out the Best Bus. On this route, the scenery of self-awareness is vast and majestic.

¡○¡ Tool! Recognize the Bus You're Riding

You might be riding the Bad Bus if

- you find yourself retelling an upsetting event to anyone and everyone—for example, if you end a long story lamenting, "And then she broke my heart," and the reaction is, "Would you like fries with that?";

- you have obsessive thoughts about a person or event; or
- you have recurrent negative thoughts about yourself, including your abilities or body image.

You can make a mental transfer to a Better Bus by

- wondering if there are other ways to look at the situation;
- challenging yourself to think about anything else—for example, doing multiplication tables or reciting a poem; or
- imagining someone you know who would have a different perspective and exploring that point of view.

You're riding the Best Bus when

- you feel a sense of excitement about something that previously upset you;
- you have an aha moment where you see new possibilities; or
- you can imagine creating new habits or behaviors and want to try them out immediately.

Who's Driving the Car?

I am laughing. Joe is not.

This doesn't bode well for the progress of the session, yet I can't contain myself. Joe and I have known one another for many years by this point. In this time, he's done stellar work and achieved many of the goals he's set for himself. We've shared a lot of laughs, and he knows I think the world of him.

I try to contain myself and manage to reign in my laughter. With a lingering smile that shows only a trace of my incredulous amusement, I tell him, "You've made a boneheaded move with disastrous consequences. That much is true. But ya gotta admit, it is humorous." Joe gives me his if-I-needed-to feel-bad-about-myself-I'd-call-my-successful-brother-who-has-no-ability to-empathize look.

"Look," I level, "your sense of humor is what gets you through the tough times. We've seen that again and again. So please don't stop laughing now. Now is also the time to remember all the happy endings you've had to other not-so-funny matters."

Even when his twelve years of marriage ended with a sudden, unexplained exit and a drained back account, we'd been able to laugh. Especially when Joe spontaneously performed a spot-on

Snagglepuss impersonation—"exit, stage left"—complete with a swoosh sound, to describe his ex-wife's rapid departure.

Laughing most of the way, Joe had turned heartache into heartfelt friendship by reaching out and building a strong network of friends. One of these new friends introduced Joe to a lovely woman who is now his kind and forthright wife and mother of their two children. From the sounds of it, the four of them laugh a lot too.

But Joe wasn't finding the humor in the events transpiring at work. He'd been having conflicts with his manager, Nate, for quite some time, and I'd suggested a few different strategies, starting with, "Don't take anything he says personally." However, that advice seemed to have failed.

Joe tells me, "My boss commented to other people on the team recently that he didn't think I was a team player, and my coworkers told me about it. You know how paranoid that makes me. Anytime a manager hasn't been upfront with me, it's meant bad news for my career."

I nod. I do know that.

Joe continues, "I kept thinking about that comment on the drive into work this morning. I've been putting in so much unpaid overtime picking up the pieces of this mismanaged project, and the more I thought about his comment, the angrier I became. Then out of the blue, I started thinking about the movie *The Green Mile*. I remembered the scene where an inmate peed on one of the guards. Later that same guard confronts the inmate and says, with a drawling southern accent, 'Piss on me? Well, piss on you.' Then he douses him with a fire hose."

Joe sighs and keeps going. "Well, I walked in this morning, and wouldn't you know it, Nate and I were the only ones in the building. Something came over me, and I walked up to him, put my laptop on his desk, slapped my ID badge on top of the computer, and said, 'Piss on you.' Then I turned around and walked out. It was only when I was outside of the building, realizing that without my badge there was no way back in, that it dawned on me: I no longer worked there.

At that point, there were only two questions in my head. First, after that confrontation, am I gonna be able to get work anywhere else? But I have a good reputation, so I think I'll be okay in the long run. Messy for now, though."

"Yes, I think that's a great question, and the correct answer too," I say supportively. "What's the second question?"

Joe looks very serious. "The second question is, did I use the accent?"

"You did," I respond without hesitation.

"How do you know?" Joe asks.

"Because you spontaneously used it while you were telling me the story. Plus, you're such a movie buff; you always use accents when you're describing scenes from a movie you watched. You also use all kinds of accents when you're describing your feelings," I reason.

"I probably did use the accent," Joe agrees, nodding his head slightly.

"But those aren't the only questions that come to my mind," I add. "Here's the first question I have for you: who was driving the car?"

"I was driving my sports ... ooooh," Joe suddenly knows what I'm talking out. "My thirteen-year-old was driving the car."

"Yes he was!" I reply enthusiastically. "And who can help put you back on the road to success?"

"My adult self," Joe mumbles, dropping his head and looking defeated.

"No need to feel defeated, Joe. C'mon, who else can help you?" I encourage.

"I don't kno— Oh! My five-year-old!" Joe exclaims.

"Excellent!"

"Wow, I just lost my job after being unemployed for almost two years, and you're so happy about it," Joe wonders.

Getting serious, I tell him, "No, I'm not happy about that. Seriously, I'm not. But I'm happy about what you can learn and how you can come out of this better off. This isn't about a new job; it's about the opportunity for you to renew your commitment to your career, starting with being very selective about who you choose to work for."

"That sounds lofty," Joe notes, unconvinced.

"Lofty? Really? For starters, I'm just hopin' you'll work in an establishment where no one gets peed on!" I joke.

Joe laughs, and that sweet sound fills the space around and between us.

"You know," he thinks aloud, "it all happened so fast that it didn't feel real to me until I returned home and the coffee machine light was still on. It has an automatic shutoff, and I hadn't even been gone long enough for it to shut off."

Knowing he's a space buff, I say, "Houston, we have a problem."

"Boy, do we," Joe agrees.

"So let's get to it."

First we review the "Who's driving the car?" concept. This tool is based on the idea that every adult has within their psyche three necessary and valuable people:

- the five-year-old self
- the thirteen-year-old self
- the adult self

Our five-year-old selves brings wonder, excitement, innocence, and joy. Our five-year-olds are very good judges of character and can "tell it like it is." Our five-year-olds may feel deeply wounded one minute but can get over it in a heartbeat. They also have the ability to forgive and extend friendship without hanging on to a grudge. Our five-year-olds sometimes suffer from fears they can't articulate and think mostly about themselves. They are concentrated on short-term goals and gains.

Our thirteen-year-old selves bring passion, independence, and pure idealistic thinking. Our thirteen-year-olds are ready to meet challenges head on. Our thirteen-year-olds aren't afraid and are ready to change the world. However, our thirteen-year-olds can also suffer from impulsive actions made with a damn-the-consequences mindset. Our thirteen-year-olds think about larger issues of justice, but mostly from the perspective of short-term goals and gains. Nevertheless, they are closer to recognizing longer-term consequences.

Our adult selves bring reason and the ability to think things through before taking action. Our adults are aware of their responsibilities and can at least manage if not embrace them. But our adult selves sometimes suffer from hanging on too long to past defeats, thereby perpetuating self-limiting messages. Our adults think about everything from many angles and are aware of balancing both short-term and long-term goals and gains.

"So what did the thirteen-year-old tell you when you decided to quit?"

"Take your f-ing job and shove it!" Joe's fists tighten as he speaks.

"Nice fists," I note. "Can you tell me what the five-year-old and adult might say?"

Joe laughs, "I got the five-year-old. He's saying, 'I don't like it, and I don't like you either.'"

I agree, "That's exactly what your five-year-old was telling you. It's important to listen to that. But your adult self also needs to come into play. So ...?"

Joe purses his lips and begins to speak but then stops. He purses his lips again, begins to speak, and then stops again.

"I can guess, if ya want," I offer.

"That'd be great."

I imagine Joe's adult self and propose, "Your adult is saying something like, 'What's done is done. Now I need to figure out how to take care of myself and my family and move things in a positive direction.'"

"Yes!" Joe is enthusiastic. "If I didn't feel like such a heel, that's what I'd be thinking!"

"Well, stop feeling like such a heel. Here are two words for you: move on! And speaking of moving on, let's get back to taking things personally," I transition.

We are both aware of Joe's history. He first came in to talk with me when he was reeling from a different job layoff. He thought he was going to spend the rest of his life at that company and was very, very (did I say very?) proud of his accomplishments there—in a super humble way. He couldn't wait for the company's next release of mobile technology. So it was quite a shock when *he* was released before the next wave of technology.

The hit to his confidence, combined with the trauma of being managed out, left him wary of managers who sacrifice employees to protect their status. Joe felt like he was in a similar situation again and thus took action (albeit drastic, self-defeating, and out-of-character action) in order to protect himself.

When I ask Joe what to call this situation, he promptly replies, "The Sucky-Job Situation." Okay, done.

I step up to the whiteboard and start to diagram the Sucky-Job Situation. Then I run through the most common human reactions when faced with unpleasant situations like this. Typically people react viscerally and think, *I don't like it!* Then they nosedive into a downward spiral of suffering. Noticing this, we think, *I've got to pull myself up by my bootstraps. I've got to get some control over this situation.* So we drag ourselves out of our despair, disappointment, and disillusionment only to arrive back at the unpleasant situation and remember, *I don't like it!* And the spiral down starts all over again.

It is precisely in these moments that I like to employ the What-It-Is tool. Instead of going up and down the spiral of despair, we can look at our situation and say, "It is what it is." This newfound perspective—which I think of as putting on outside observer glasses—let's us take a good look at the consequences of our current situation.

🍴 Tool! What It Is and What I'd Prefer

In Joe's Sucky-Job Situation, here are the consequences we identified:

- not feeling appreciated for his hard work and dedication
- working unpaid overtime
- job-related stress that impacts his family life
- limited job satisfaction
- lack of teamwork
- tough relationship with manager
- a paltry paycheck that just barely allows him to support his family

Sometimes after taking an honest look at the consequences we can identify one aspect that's so important it outweighs all the negatives. In Joe's case, a paycheck that allows him to support his family could have been important enough to continue in his sucky job until something better came along. However, in order to move forward, it's vital to identify what that something better would look like. This is a great opportunity to put on our outside-observer glasses and ask ourselves, "What would I prefer?" This can be an exciting step, and at this point many of my clients experience a surge of new ideas and courage.

Using this tool, Joe realizes that instead of his Sucky-Job Situation, he would much prefer

- to be in an environment where he could do his best work;
- to feel like he's part of a strong, hardworking, and fun-loving team;
- to receive appreciation for his work;
- to earn a great paycheck;
- to have a better work/life balance;
- to get and give support on his team;
- to produce an exceptional product;
- to be supported for his abilities to create diligent workflow processes; and
- to give something great to the world!

Once Joe is able to see his Sucky-Job Situation clearly, he gets excited about finding the right working environment. Instead of feeling like a victim to a power-hungry, demanding, and demeaning manager, he feels empowered by knowing what he wants and having the freedom to find it.

Years later, Joe has created his own business that combines technology, aviation, and movies. He manages an amazing team and no longer needs to play out scenes from someone else's show, though he still does sometimes, just for grins.

"Joe, this is great! How did you put it all together?" I marvel.

He smiles and adopts a drawling southern accent, "I just figured out who needed to drive the car."

"You know you used the accent," I tease, referring to the day that ultimately led to so much positive change.

"You know you helped me out when I was down," Joe replies, maintaining the accent.

"My pleasure, Joe."

¡◯¡ Tool! Pros and Cons of Your Three Personal Drivers:

We each have three versions of ourselves inside our psyches. Together they can help us make the best decisions and formulate the best plan of action. Knowing each one's strengths and weaknesses can help us decide who should be in the driver's seat and who can provide helpful information to the driver.

Our five-year-old selves:

Pros	Cons
Embrace a sense of wonder, joy, excitement, and innocence	Think mostly about themselves
Can tell it like it is	Can only tell it like it is
Good judge of character	Focused on short-term needs
Able to forgive and move forward in friendships	Can be easily and deeply wounded

Our thirteen-year-old selves:

Pros	Cons
Embrace a sense of passion, independence, and pure idealistic thinking	Can be extremely impulsive; don't always think through the consequences of their actions, or ignore consequences in favor of high-risk behaviors

145

| Meet challenges head on | Focused on short-term goals and gains |
| Ready to change the world | In the process of developing a strong but often immature sense of justice |

Our adult selves:

Pros	Cons
Embrace a sense of reason and rational thinking	Can use fear to limit imagination
Able to think things through and manage responsibilities	Can suffer from past defeats and self-limiting beliefs
Can think in terms of both short- and long-term goals and gains	Can have a difficult time forgiving others and moving forward in relationships

What to Do When Life Throws You a Curve Ball

Natalie is a mess. This is understandable, considering life has just thrown her a curve ball.

"My manager wasn't the only one. Three of my best friends at work also threw the tricky pitch," she sobs from beneath her company baseball cap. Her usually calm voice is gone, and her giant, doe-like brown eyes are overflowing with tears. She keeps talking though, even as she delicately reaches for the box of Kleenex I'd moved closer to her.

"I was just starting to really like work and to have fun with my coworkers—you know, joke around a little. I trusted one person with personal feelings, and … and …" She stops talking and lets out a deep sigh, dotting the tissue under her eyes and along her cheeks. "I know I can find other work, but still, it's so disappointing to be laid off and told I wasn't making the cut when just a week ago the same manager praised my work."

Paula is one of my spunkiest clients. At seventeen she suffered from a nearly paralyzing back injury. Not only was she able to learn to walk again, but she went on to become an honors student and a three-sport athlete. She's fearless. And fired.

"They threw me a curve ball," she reports. "It was bogus. My manager text-messaged me to ask for my office key. He didn't even have the guts to fire me to my face! Why was I fired? What could I have done better? Who knows? And just so you know, I don't need you to think I'm great or anything, but honestly, I was a superior employee. I miss my coworkers, but who wants to stay someplace where they treat you like that?"

I could also write all day about Natalie or Paula—their disappointments, anger, and dives into self-doubt. But what each of their stories has in common is a curve ball. You've got your eyes on the pitch and are ready to swing when the ball takes a dive. In terms of life, a curve ball is anything that brings a significant and unexpected divergence from the path you thought you were following.

So how can you recover when life throws you a curve ball? I'm glad you asked because, voila! Here's an iron-clad, six-step process for recovering your amazing self.

🍴 Tool! Six Steps to Regain Balance When Life Throws You a Curve Ball

Recognize: You've been thrown a curve ball in the game of life! Ambushed! Hit by a sniper! Acknowledge all of the feelings that go along with this (hint: pain, sadness, incredulity, anger, vengeance, and self-doubt).

Learn: What can you learn from this situation? Specifically, what changes can you immediately start implementing in your attitude or behavior? For instance, Natalie learned that in order to avoid the perception of "speaking with a harsh tone," she could ask questions instead of making statements. For example, instead of saying, "We're really behind, and there's a customer who's been waiting thirty-five minutes for you," she could inquire, "Were you aware that one of our customers has been waiting for thirty-five minutes?"

Act: Hold your head up high and do great work. This is necessary for your sense of integrity. Start by being a great spouse, a great friend, or both. Shore up any areas where you've let commitments to yourself or others slide. Then recommit and take the best possible action. Then take the next and the next ... you get the idea.

Forgive: Forgive others for their bad boundaries, bad behaviors, or both so that you can move on. Holding on to perceived slights creates a giant iceberg in our insides, causing us to become tense and coloring our experiences with icy-blue depression. But forgiving isn't forgetting. In this case, it is the acknowledgement that all people make mistakes. Make a consistent effort to forgive the person who threw you the curve ball. Somewhat surprisingly—especially to most Westerners—forgiveness most benefits the one who offers it. Forgiveness breaks down the thick walls of hurt and resentment, thereby allowing positive feelings about life to flow.

Share: There is always the possibility of talking with those who threw you the curve ball if those people are important to you—such as a beloved spouse, a respected manager, or wonderful friend. You can share with them positive and heartfelt feelings. For example, "I really enjoyed the closeness we shared, and I'd like to promote that again. I'm open to any ideas you might have" Or, "It's important to me that you understand I'm a truthful person/hard worker/dedicated spouse. I'd like to help restore any trust that's been lost due to this misunderstanding, because I believe our connection is worth fighting for."

Express Gratitude: The best way to move forward after being thrown a curve ball is to focus on what good things remain in your life. Who are the people you can trust? What lessons about how to treat (or not treat) others have you learned? What opportunities can open up for you because of this experience? Could this be a time to look for new work or new friends or finally decide to put the energy of your entire being into an oft-postponed dream? As you answer these questions while leaning into a deep sense of gratitude, watch poison turn into passion.

How to Become a Beautiful Sunflower of Imperfect Perfection

"I never qualify for college grants, so I stopped applying for them—and to college," Janie explains.

"I never seem to get the job I want, so I decided I'm going to be one of those worker bees who just keeps going in the job I've got," Jim says resignedly.

"I never date the kind of person I dream of being with, so I guess I'll make peace with being single," say Lily, Lyle, Joan, and John.

I feel sorry for these people. Not for the reasons you might be thinking, but because there is something they all share in common: each of them is going to hear "The Seed Story." While I am enamored with "The Seed Story," many clients are not. Not at first telling, that is. It's a story that has to grow on you.

I always start the same way, by reaching for a beautiful, mammoth sunflower that sits in a vase in my office. "This sunflower came from my garden," I tell them. "I've been raising them for years—planting the seeds in the ground and then watching and waiting and watering. Watching and waiting and watering."

At this early point in "The Seed Story," I notice the dull, blank stare on my clients' faces. I can "hear" the internal dialogue that pleads, in vain, to make it stop. Make. It. Stop. Yet I'm still talking about watching, waiting, and watering. Finally, I move on.

I tell them that eventually, out of nowhere, beautiful buds appear on the plants. Most sunflower buds will take up to a week or longer to completely unfold. During the process, the personality of each flower is clearly revealed. Some explode with a few petals at a time, looking angry at the world for the unpleasantness of the process. Others unwrap slowly, gently opening to the world with a sense of trust and awe. Still others burst forth in a semi-open position as they reconsider this "fully blossoming" proposition. A few open easily, with a steady inner rhythm that greets the new world. At this point, I am so into the story, and my clients can barely conceal their disdain. I can "hear" their continuing inner dialogue, which sounds like, *I bet you're also the crazy cat woman in your neighborhood.*

Perfect! I think. I've seen this moment over and over again. We are right where we need to be in the therapeutic process, because now I'm going to say something that will surprise my clients and touch on part of the root of why they are here.

"The point of all this unfolding is to let you know that however you are unfolding, it's okay. Because here is what happens, year after year, in a very dependable way, each and every one of the seeds becomes a beautiful sunflower of imperfect perfection." I hold up the giant sunflower, which can measure between seven and fourteen inches in diameter, and marvel. "This flower started from this." I gently show off a sunflower seed that is just 0.7 inches in diameter.

"The Seed Story' teaches us that growth requires patience, effort, love, and vision. These are all things you're capable of. So no matter how small you feel —here I hold up the seed again—"we know how large you and your life can become." I show off the gorgeous sunflower once more before returning it to the vase.

This turns the tide, and now the client is all questions. "Tell me more!"

"Well, when I first started growing sunflowers, I was sort of surprised to see that the seeds really were sunflower seeds, like the kind I used to eat as a kid. Then I planted the seeds in the ground. What do you suppose happened next?" I ask.

"They grew?" the client will venture.

"No. What happened next was nothing. Nothing happened. Nothing that I could see, that is."

"Well, then what happened?" Yes, despite previously wanting to run screaming from my office, the client is now totally engrossed.

"Then something exciting happened," I continue. "The first light-green sprouts broke free through the dirt. They were so tender."

"That's so cool!" the client exclaims. "Then what?"

"Then it's not so cool. I noticed that the plants were not very strong. I was giving them a lot of love—clearing out the weeds, making sure they got lots of water, and so on—but I was really worried. You just really can't tell at this point if they're going to make it," I caution.

"What did you do to help the plants make it?" the client wants to know.

"I gave them more love, more weeding, and more water. I kept on making the same consistent efforts, no matter how strong or weak the plant looked," I reply.

"Oh." Clients are smart. At this point they begin to see the parallels. "Then what?" they ask hesitantly.

"Well, this is the good part," I say. "One day I looked out at the plants and noticed that they had become strong. They had robust stalks that started growing at an amazingly rapid speed, shooting out of the ground and soaring toward the sky!"

"That's great," says the relieved client.

"The next part is what we've been waiting for: each plant brought forth a sunflower, and each one was beautiful and unique. It was so fun to enjoy each one for its distinct character."

"Hmm," says the client. "I'd almost forgotten about the actual flower."

"That's because you were actively involved in imagining the process. Once you got into the process, you naturally stopped focusing so much on the results," I observe.

One of my favorite clients, upon reaching this point in the story, told me, "You're crazy like the fox."

"Ah, Grasshopper, you think the story has ended, but it still has a second half!" I note serenely.

"I was afraid of that," my clients usually respond. "So what else?"

"This story also illustrates the concept of inherent potential," I reveal. "While the seeds never would have grown into flowers without my help, each sunflower seed already possessed the inherent potential for a flower. In a similar way, when the flowers did finally blossom, their beauty was limitless, and they filled me with joy every time I saw them. In other words, the plants activated my 'happy system'—that is, the inherent capacity for joy that all human beings possess. And the happier I felt, the more love, joy, and beauty I could share with others.

"But it's also important to note that both the plants and I had to focus on making consistent effort and not get discouraged by what was happening in the moment. The first day after I planted the seeds, I didn't look out and say, 'I don't see any flowers! What a waste of effort! I'm done trying.' Yet as human beings, we often do this with our goals; we stop taking action and abandon them to wilt way too early on. It was the constancy and consistency of my effort, as well as the effort of the sunflowers, that led to this amazing outcome. The seeds kept striving to grow and become strong plants, and I stayed diligent in my efforts to"—here the client sometimes joins in—"watch, wait, and water."

After a few seconds of taking it all in, the client usually responds, "Got it."

So I continue. "If you only focus on getting the grant, having the new job, or meeting the perfect person, you'll miss the real lesson. While the end result can be amazing—often beyond our wildest dreams—and is ours to be enjoyed, it is the continual and consistent effort itself that brings true joy. Because by the end, what we're proudest of isn't the material reward, it's actually winning in our internal struggle."

I pause, breathe deeply a couple of times, and wait for any questions or comments—which never come at this point in the session. Then I continue. "I can't force you to keep applying to colleges and scholarships, to keep looking for the best career fit, or to keep searching for your imperfectly-perfect partner. However, I can ask that you reconsider giving up."

The "Seed Story" session is one of the few in which I do most of the talking. Yet after a little bit of disgruntled, my-counselor-doesn't-get-me grumbling, my clients settle in, enjoy the story, and live out the lessons.

Later on, Janie excitedly reports, "I found the best college for me, and I was offered a scholarship that covers half of my tuition."

Jim shares, "I knew I wanted a different job; I just didn't realize that I'd have to become stronger to get it. Now I'm excited about going to work and want to become an even better me."

"I sometimes miss being single. No, not really. Just kidding! I'm so in love with my fabulous partner!" say Lily, Lyle, Joan, and John.

🍴 Tool! Get That Goal

- Never give up on your goals and dreams. If it is important to you, it's important.
- Seeds do not sprout into flowers immediately. Be patient with yourself and your dreams. Do not despair; instead, keep going.
- Achieving your desired result comes from continuous effort.
- Focus on the efforts you can and need to make in the present moment.
- Sincere efforts will always add up. The important thing is to make the effort no matter what results you've had in

the past. Today is a new day and a new opportunity; this represents a new effort.

- To become happy, tend to the seeds (goals, dreams, desires, passions, etc.) in your garden with love and care.

Afterword

From the beginning, I was a girl who dreamed in written stories, and I often awoke surprised and laughing at my own imagination. I've been writing for my entire life, even though this is my first published work. Yet, a passion for stories is part of my makeup.

As a licensed counselor, I wake up every day ready to hear stories of courage, hurt, sadness, fear, fierce determination, clarity, growth, and connection. Fortunately, I have turned this passion into a career.

But it wasn't easy. I fought for twenty years to develop my career into one that supported me and helped me give my best to every single client. During that time, there were moments, actually years, when I felt like a failure.

Call me a late bloomer, but I never gave up on the belief that each of us could earn a decent living, make our unique contribution to society, and feel refreshed—not exhausted—in the process. I was also fortunate to have the support of amazing people who believed in me even when I doubted myself. And by "believed in me," I mean shoved me off the cliff of my comfort zone, which I might not have appreciated so much at the time.

I didn't used to think I could give a keynote address or plan a weeklong training course, but it turns out I can. And you know what's even better? These events, time after time, pushed me to expand my capacity and have inspired each participant to do the same.

These days I support private clients in one-on-one and couples-therapy sessions, give keynote speeches, and deliver personalized training workshops for companies, nonprofits, and schools. I'm based in Woodinville, Washington, but I happily travel to domestic and international locations.

My professional goal is to help all my clients—each person, couple, organization, or company—understand that they have unlimited potential, limited only by their beliefs.

If I can run a successful business and feel the deepest of joys doing it, you can do anything - set your mind and you will accomplish it. So, go do it! Get started. And spread joy and compassion as you go.

I hope you've had a great experience reading the stories in this book. I wrote them with the sole purpose of serving you, so I hope you've made them your own. I would love to hear about your experiences with the tools and stories in this book, as well as any general reactions or realizations.

You can reach me at robin@RobinMorrisCounseling.com and at RobinRaeMorris.com

Also, for book and services information, please visit www. robinraemorris.com.